Alexander Hume

Songs and Poems, Chiefly Scottish

Third Edition

Alexander Hume

Songs and Poems, Chiefly Scottish
Third Edition

ISBN/EAN: 9783744775458

Printed in Europe, USA, Canada, Australia, Japan

Cover: Foto ©Thomas Meinert / pixelio.de

More available books at **www.hansebooks.com**

CHIEFLY

SCOTTISH

BY

ALEXANDER HUME

With a Glossary

THIRD EDITION

LONDON
SAMPSON LOW, MARSTON, SEARLE, & RIVINGTON
Limited
St. Dunstan's House
FETTER LANE, FLEET STREET, E.C.
1890
[*All rights reserved*]

TO

HIS EARLY AND TRUE HEARTED FRIEND,

RICHARD TWENTYMAN,

THIS EDITION OF SONGS AND POEMS IS AFFECTIONATELY DEDICATED

BY THE AUTHOR.

urge in my defence is, that it was to them that my songs (such as they are) owed their birth. I love the melodies of our country—enthusiastically love them. The crooning them over at home and abroad—in the city and the field—engendered corresponding sentiments in my mind; and it was my aim, in giving those sentiments expression, to clothe them in the simple and appropriate language of our native land. In short, I have endeavoured to make them natural; and, of all poetical compositions, songs, at least those of the affections, should be so. Warm gushes of feeling —brief, simple, and condensed—as soon as they have left the singer's lips they should be fast round the hearer's heart, there to dwell, not live and die in a sound.

Perhaps they may strike a sympathetic chord in the bosom of some more ruled by nature than by art; if they do so, I shall be glad. If any receive but one half the pleasure in reading them, or in hearing them sung, that I did in writing them, they will indeed have much, and I shall be happy.

I am, my dear Sir,

Yours most truly,

ALEXANDER HUME.

PREFACE

TO THE

FIRST EDITION OF ENGLISH SONGS AND BALLADS.

TO

W. J. Fox, Esq.

MY DEAR SIR,—I dedicated my former volume of Scottish Songs to ALLAN CUNNINGHAM, the Biographer of Robert Burns, because I received great kindness at his hands, both as a man and an author. As I am greatly your debtor, I feel much pleasure in taking the only opportunity I have of expressing my sense of the obligation, by dedicating this volume to you.

My former Songs were wedded to the melodies of my native land—a land rich in melodies that have outlived the discord of centuries, not in moth-decayed manuscripts, or in costly folios, but in the hearts alike of noble and peasant; in the cottage and in the palace; ever fresh and sweet, never dying or growing old.

Song, of all descriptions of poetry, is a powerful agent in holding the minds of men for good or evil, as it may be directed. Some one said that he cared not who made the laws of the country so long as he made the songs, and it was a beautiful saying, yet not more beautiful than it was true; for, however much society is benefited by the law, still its object is to force man to justice, while the true object of Song is to draw him to it, for the love of it. Let those sneer at this who never heard or felt a song, beyond the compositions so called, that fall from the press in scores weekly, whose principal merit, if merit they have, lies in the lithographed title-page generally attached to them. They are not songs, but meaningless words attached to meaningless sounds, on which fashion has set its seal, to amuse or surprise a meaningless audience. A true song is a hymn breathed out from the lowest depths of the heart, and, like electricity on the air, stirring all that comes within its influence. It is not at home in the drawing-room, comes not at request, but is ever spontaneous. The head may entreat, ay, command, and the lips send forth words and sounds, but if the heart wills it not, it is the pipe without a player; the spirit is not there. When the heart is full it runs over, and finds relief in the dear joy of its own flowing. It has beguiled many and many a weary hour of its sorrows, and made doubly full many a happy one, and when heard issuing from the lips of some rustic maiden, wedded to some beautiful melody, fit companion for such beautiful truth, and drawing forth the sympathies of the listeners around her, let those who witness it, and it can be witnessed at every cotter's fire, and on every hill-side in Scotland, deny, if they can, that Song, in its influence, is mighty deep, and enduring.

Here is a proof of its power, as related by the late lamented Robert Nicholl, author of a volume of beautiful Lyrics. "During the expedition to Buenos Ayres, a Highland soldier, while a prisoner in the hands of the Spaniards, having formed an attachment to a woman of the country, and charmed by the easy life which the tropical fertility of the soil enabled the inhabitants to lead, had resolved to remain and settle in South America. When he imparted this resolution to his comrade, the latter did not argue with him, but leading him to his tent, he placed him by his side, and sung him 'Lochabar no more:' the spell was on him, the tears came into his eyes, and wrapping his beautiful and very popular words, the reader or hearer found it difficult to think of the melody, without associating the old composition with it; and knowing no original airs that would suit my purpose, and of which I could take advantage, I have risked the publication of these lyrics in their present shape in the hope that they may be acceptable without the aid of music.

Those who never take up a book except to pass away a lazy hour will, I fear, find much disappointment in these compositions,—they are not adapted, nor were they written for such, but for those who think and feel for themselves; whatever they look on, look for instruction, and when they receive it, impart it to their brothers, and do *something* towards making their fellow-creatures wiser, and consequently happier; drawing men into one family, one mighty head, and one universal heart.

To those who may feel inclined to carp at the faulty expression or construction that, I have no doubt, will be found in the small volume, I can only say that I have had little "school" experience to produce it. "My heart ran o'er, and found relief in the dear joy of its own flowing."

I remain, my dear Sir,
Yours most sincerely,
ALEXANDER HUME.

CONTENTS.

SONGS.

MY LOVE IS LIKE MY AIN COUNTRIE.
My love is like my ain countrie . . . 1

MY WEE WEE WIFE.
My wee wife dwells in yonder cot . . 2

O POVERTY.
Eliza was a bonnie lass, and oh! she lo'ed me weel

THE BLINK O' A BONNIE BRIGHT E'E.
Sweet is the heather when it is bloomin' 5

SANDY ALLAN.
Wha is he I hear sae crouse .

THE TWO GRAVES.
Two bodies in a churchyard lay . 7

MY BONNIE JEAN.
O my Jean, my bonnie, bonnie Jean

CONTENTS.

	PAGE
I MAUN LEAVE YE.	
An' I maun leave ye, bonnie quean	9
THE WIFE O' ELDERSLIE.	
O nature! why hae you me gi'en	10
THE TWEED.	
My auld bonnie Tweed rin on, aye may ye rin as clear	11
SHE'S SWEET, SHE'S FAIR.	
She's sweet, she's fair, an' oh! she's dear	12
OH! DOOL ON THE DAY I WAS MARRIED.	
Oh! dool on the day, oh! dool on the day	13
YE FATHERS.	
Ye fathers wha worship the penny siller	14
* WHAT AM I?	
What am I that I should bow	15
* MILLICENT MORAN.	
Young Millicent Moran was married in May	16
* OH! WHAT ARE FRIENDS?	
Oh! what are friends, the best, the nearest	17
NANNY.	
There's mony a flow'r beside the rose	18
I CANNA LIE.	
I canna lie, I canna gang	18
MY BESSIE.	
My Bessie, oh! but look upon these bonnie budding flow'rs	19

CONTENTS.

	PAGE
AN AULD MAN'S SONG.	
Oh! lead me where the wild flow'rs grow	20
DOCTOR O'SLEE.	
Oh! heard ye the like o't in countrie or toon?	22
THE WIND BLAWS CAULDLY.	
The wind blaws cauldly through the door	23
OH! MICKLE BEAUTY.	
Oh! mickle beauty, love is thine	24
JEAN SITS ON YON HILLOCK.	
Jean sits on yon hillock a' the lang day	25
HOW SWEET TO HEAR.	
How sweet to hear a melody o' our ain land!	25
A CARLE CAM TO OUR HA' GATE.	
A carle cam to our ha' gate	26
* MY OLD WIFE.	
My old wife has neither grace	28
THE BRAES O' TWEEDALE.	
My blessing on the bonny braes	29
* MY SWEET LASSIE.	
Oh! but look on my sweet lassie	30
* WHY DO YE TARRY.	
Why do ye tarry	31
THE LAD WHA'LL SOON BE FAR AWA'.	
A' ye wha ever grasped the hand	32

CONTENTS.

	PAGE
MENIE HAY.	
A wee bird sits upon a spray	33
FAREWELL TO THE LAND.	
Farewell to the land of our fathers, farewell !	34
* I'VE LOVED THEE.	
I've loved thee, love, long; I've loved thee, love, deep .	35
WATTY'S WEDDING.	
There ne'er was seen sic sport and play .	36
ELIZA.	
Oh! fragrant ever be the dell	37
IF THERE WERE FEELING.	
If there were feeling in the air . . .	38
ONE EVENING.	
One evening in the bright moonlight .	39
YE BONNY SUN.	
Oh! shine away ye bonny sun . .	40
WHEN SUMMER DAYS.	
When summer days were in their prime . .	41
A MINSTREL.	
A minstrel sang in a garden bower . .	42
* MY WIFIE WEE.	
My wifie wee	44
JESSY RAE.	
Bonnie Jessy Rae, wi' mind love has birth	45

CONTENTS. xix

PAGE

*CAN I FORGET?
Can I forget what once I've seen . . 45

A HEALTH TO HIM WHO THINKS.
While princes rule by whip and steel . 46

A COTTER I.
A cotter I, wha ne'er deny . . . 47

MY BONNIE WEE NANNY.
My bonnie wee Nanny, my blessings be on ye . 48

TO MY WIFE.
We'll not go nigh the sight to-day . . . 49

THERE'S JOY NAE MAIR IN ANNIE'S E'E.
There's joy nae mair in Annie's e'e . . . 50

MY JEANNIE.
O fa', fa', ye showers 51

JOCK'S WIFE.
What din is that in yon house? 52

THE BARD.
It was upon a winter's day 53

WHEN FLOWERS.
When flowers were in their fairest bloom . . 55

KING MIND.
A health unto the king 55

I'VE WANDERED ON THE SUNNY HILL.
I've wandered on the sunny hill, I've wandered in the vale 56

CONTENTS.

	PAGE
MY MOUNTAIN HAME.	
My mountain hame! my mountain hame!	57

POEMS.

* INTRODUCTION TO A POEM.	
When summer shed its beauty o'er the land	59
* ON THE DEATH OF ROBERT NICHOLL.	
O Death! ye play a mournfu' part	70
* PRAYER OF A COLOURED MAN.	
Great Father of this beauteous earth	73
* A PASSING QUESTION.	
To whom place you a statue there	75
THOUGHT.	
Though patrons shun my house and name	76
LOVE'S CRUELTY.	
Love, close those eyes, they pain me sore	77
EVIDENCE OF LOVE.	
Oh! why am I thus happy made?	78
PHILOSOPHY OF LOVE.	
Ah! why thy face in sorrow clad?	78
LOVE'S DYING.	
If love can fade, let heavy life	79
* TO MY CHILD THAT LIVETH STILL.	
My baby, they say thou art gone	80

CONTENTS

	PAGE
THE BEGGAR AND HIS BROTHER.	
Good friend, come wander down the vale	81
TRUTH.	
Come sit thee down, and we will sing	83
* VERSES WRITTEN AFTER HEARING "RULE BRITANNIA" SUNG.	
Oh! never sing of ruling wide	84
CANDOUR.	
Shalt thou give pain unto thy heart	85
A CAUTION.	
Pass by the maid without a heart	86
TO MOURNERS.	
Why mock thy friend with sighs and tears	87
TO MY PEN.	
I cannot think, poor pen, not I	87
LOVE.	
Were my dear love the balmy air	88
A COMPANY.	
The hall was filled, the wine went round	88
SONG OF A DRINKER.	
There's not a man this day alive	90
DEVOTION.	
I never knew that life was sweet	91

CONTENTS.

	PAGE
THE TUNE OF GALLA WATER.	
Of tunes that with my heart accord	92
DEAR LOVE.	
Dear love, wilt thou go to the fields with me?	93
MY BOOKS.	
Some love to gaze on beauty's face	94

Those Songs and Poems marked with an Asterisk (*) were not printed in the former Editions.

SONGS.

MY LOVE IS LIKE MY AIN COUNTRIE.

Air—" My Love is like a red, red rose."

My Love is like my ain countrie,
That to my heart is dear;
My Love is like the holly tree,
That's green through a' the year;
Her smile is like the glowing ray
That fa's from yonder sun:
And, sunlike, blesses a' the day,
Yet kens nae gude she's done.

Her lips hae named the bridal time,
Her lips hae sealed the vow;
Like Nature's laws in every clime
We'll aye be true as now.
Like Nature, love the fairer grows
The mair we ken its law;
Like air it through the warld flows,
Sweet harmony to a'.

Oh! fly ye lazy, listless hours,
And bring that happy day,
When we'll in wedlock's sweetest bow'rs
In love kiss life away.
We'll live like sleepers in a dream,
Where wishes paint the scene,
And care shall melt by pleasure's beam
As snow melts on the green.

MY WEE WEE WIFE.

Air—"*The Boatie rows.*"

My wee wife dwells in yonder cot,
My bonnie bairnies three,
Oh! happy is the husband's lot,
Wi' bairnies on his knee.
My wee wee wife, my wee wee wife,
My bonnie bairnies three;
How bright is day! how sweet is life!
When love lights up the e'e.

The king o'er me, may wear a crown
Have millions bow the knee,
But lacks he love to share his throne,
How poor a king is he!
My wee wee wife, my wee wee wife,
My bonnie bairnies three,
Let kings hae thrones, 'mang warld's strife,
Your hearts are thrones to me.

I've felt oppression's galling chain,
I've shed the tear o' care ;
But feeling aye lost a' its pain,
When my wee wife was near.
My wee wee wife, my wee wee wife,
My bonnie bairnies three,
The chains we wear are sweet to bear,
How sad, could we go free !

I've mony seen amang the crowd,
Laid by misfortune low ;
I've mony years on time seen row'd,
And mony changes grow ;
But my wee wife, my dear wee wife,
My bonnie bairnies three,
I never saw the daylight da'
That bless'd not you and me.

O POVERTY !

Air—*The Posie.*

Eliza was a bonnie lass, and oh ! she lo'ed me weel,
Sic love as canna find a tongue, but only hearts can feel ;
But I was poor, her father doure, he wadna look on me,
O Poverty ! O Poverty ! that love should bow to thee.

I went unto her mother, and I argued and I fleeched,
I spak' o' love and honesty, and mair and mair beseeched ;

But she was deaf to a' my grief, she wadna look on me,
O Poverty! O Poverty! that love should bow to thee.

I next went to her brother, and I painted a' my pain,
I told him o' our plighted troth, but it was a' in vain;
Tho' he was deep in love himsel' nae feeling he'd for me,
O Poverty! O Poverty! that love should bow to thee.

Oh! wealth it makes the fool a sage, the knave an honest man,
And cankered grey locks young again, if he has gear and lan';
To age maun beauty ope her arms, tho' wi' a tearfu' e'e,
O Poverty! O Poverty! that love should bow to thee.

But wait a wee, oh! love is slee, and winna be said nay,
It breaks a' chains, except its ain, but it will hae its way;
In spite o' fate we took the gate, now happy as can be,
O Poverty! O Poverty! we're wed in spite o' thee.

THE BLINK O' A BONNIE BRIGHT E'E.

Air—"*Saw ye my wee thing.*"

Sweet is the heather when it is bloomin';
Sweet is the scent o' the hawthorn tree;
Sweet are the lips and the tresses o' woman,
Sweeter the blink o' her bonnie bright e'e.
'Tis not its boldness, 'tis not its coldness;
But 'tis—in truth I canna tell thee—
Softly beseeching, slee and bewitching,
Sweet is the blink o' a bonnie bright e'e.

Sweet 'tis to look on the roses' blossom,
Sweet when the sunbeams are kissing its bree,
While May is wreathing, while perfume breathing,
Over the mountain and over the lea.
But meikle fairer are roses and rarer,
Fair are their hues and lovely to see,
While they are teeming, with warm rays beaming,
From the sweet blink o' a bonnie bright e'e.

Sweet 'tis to feel it, sweet 'tis to tell it,
Hard 'tis to wander near it and gang free.
Tho' it is ruin, bless we our undoin',
And melt in the blink o' a bonnie bright e'e.
When mother Nature formed her first creature,
Waesome was he, ungainly to see;
Unfit for his station—to rule o'er creation—
She gave him the blink o' a bonnie bright e'e.

SANDY ALLAN.

Air—"Fee him Father."

Wha is he I hear sae crouse,
There behind the hallan;
Whose skirling rings thro' a' the house,
Ilk corner o' the dwallin'?
Oh! it is ane, a merry chiel,
As mirth e'er set a bawlin',
Or filled a neuk in drouthy biel,
It's canty Sandy Allan,
    Canty,
Canty Sandy Allan.

He has a gaucy kind gudewife,
This blythesome Sandy Allan,
Wha lo'es him mickle mair than life,
And glories in her callan.
As sense and sound are ane in sang,
Sae Jean and Sandy Allan,
Twa hearts yet but ae pulse and tongue,
Has Luckie and her callan,
    Luckie,
Luckie and her callan.

To gie to a' it's aye his rule
Their proper name and callin',
A knave's a knave, a fool's a fool
Wi' honest Sandy Allan.

For every vice he has a dart,
And heavy is its fallin' ;
But aye for worth a kindred heart,
Has ever Sandy Allan,
    Ever,
Ever Sandy Allan.

To kings his knee he wunna bring,
Sae proud is Sandy Allan,
The man who thinks and feels is king—
A god—wi' Sandy Allan.
Auld Nature, just to show the warl'
Ae truly honest callan,
She strippit till't and made the carle,
And ca'd him Sandy Allan,
    Ca'd him,
Ca'd him Sandy Allan.

THE TWO GRAVES.

Set to an original air by the author, and published by Jefferys & Co., Soho Square.]

Two bodies in a churchyard lay,
Fast sleeping in their graves,
Beyond the pale of passion's sway
Of life's tumultuous waves.
The one of these two beings freed,
A Christian lived and died ;
The other held the Koran creed,
And the two slept side by side.

The Christian had been hearsed along,
Mourned by sigh and tear ;
And reverend lips a requiem sung,
Over the Christian bier.

But he of Koran creed was borne
As carrion to the grave,
Unwept, unsung ; for who would mourn
A crossless Koran slave ?

As time rolled on, these two graves were
All covered o'er with flow'rs,
That smelt as sweet, and bloomed as fair,
As they had sprung in bow'rs.
'Twas beautiful the flow'rs to bloom
Upon the Christian grave ;
But then to deck the church-bann'd tomb
Of that unchristian slave.

In that churchyard I strayed to view
The two graves side by side ;
And flow'rs as fresh as if they grew
To grace some new-made bride.
I asked how clay of Christian slept
Beside a Koran slave's,
The wind alone from silence crept,
The wind sung o'er the graves.

MY BONNIE JEAN.

Air—*Broom o' the Cowdenas.*

O my Jean, my bonnie, bonnie Jean,
My ain dear Jean alway,
Ten years together we have seen,
They seem but ae short day.
    O my Jean,
My bonnie, bonnie Jean.

O my Jean, my bonnie, bonnie Jean,
I wonder how it can be,
Ye think the wee things like me gi'en,
When they're sae like to thee.
    O my Jean,
My bonnie, bonnie Jean.

O my Jean, my bonnie, bonnie Jean,
Folk talk o' their youthfu' time,
it's only when our hearts are keen,
That we are in our prime.
    O my Jean,
My bonnie, bonnie Jean.

O my Jean, my bonnie, bonnie Jean,
When cometh the must come day,
We'll smile farewell on life's fair scene,
And, sunlike, gang our way.
    O my Jean,
My bonnie, bonnie Jean.

I MAUN LEAVE YE.

AIR—"*An' ye shall walk in silk attire.*"

An' I maun leave ye bonnie quean,
It's mair than I can bear;
When to another ye are gi'en,
I ne'er shall see ye mair.
But how, oh! how can I depart,
Unless that I could dee,
When ye've a pris'ner made my heart,
Nor can I rend it free?

An' ye'll gae meet another's kiss,
An' ye'll to him be true;
Will mem'ry never mar the bliss,
Between your love an' you?
Oh! ye maun think poor love's a flower,
That blooms but to decay,
Which ye may pu' at any hour,
To crush an' fling away.

My bonnie lass, e'en gang your way,
An' lie doon by his side;
Ye'll pray for him ye've scorned to-day,
When you're a wedded bride.
Love lies no in a honey smile,
Nor yet in a bright e'e;
An' when ye've found they've been your guile,
Oh! then ye'll think o' me.

THE WIFE O' ELDERSLIE.

AIR—"*My only Jo and dearie O!*"

O NATURE! why hae you me gi'en,
A heart to feel, an' e'e to see?
Oh! why to life send such a quean,
As she, the wife o' Elderslie?
Let me gae read, let me gae sing,
She's in my book, my melodie,
My dazzled e'en drink in the scene
But the sweet wife o' Elderslie.

Oh! weel she lo'es her auld gudeman,
Oh! weel the bairnie on her knee;
An' strang's the chain that binds the twain,
The man an' wife o' Elderslie.
Tho' twa score winters he has seen,
An' barely twenty summers she,
When hearts are keen, then years are green,
An' green the years o' Elderslie.

Ye pow'rs above, on her look doon,
An' aye from ill preserve her free,
The poorest fen to guard their kin,
Guard you the wife o' Elderslie.
If marriage bonds are made on high,
I pray when ye provide for me,
Be your decree as fair a she,
The sweet, sweet wife o' Elderslie.

THE TWEED.

[Set to an old Scottish Melody, is published by Jefferys & Co., Soho Square.]

My auld bonnie Tweed rin on, aye may ye rin as clear
As you do now, my mother stream, for mony coming year;
May ilka bonnie flow'r that blooms, may ilka bloomless weed,
That near ye grows, aye pray wi' me for blessings on the Tweed.

The gowan nestles on your banks, there stands the
 stately tree,
The sheep an' kye aft wander there, there sips the
 honey bee,
The sonsy lassies bleach their claes beside you in
 the mead,
An' as your waters fa' in show'rs, sing blessings on
 the Tweed.

The patient fisher watches you wi' weather-beaten
 frame,
An' mickle lippens he to you for happy house an'
 hame,
How mony thankfu' hearts ye make! how mony
 mou's ye feed!
The very wee things lisping cry for blessings on
 the Tweed.

Upon your banks I drew my breath, your course
 I've wandered thro',
An' love for nature grew wi' me, as my love grew
 for you,
Ye fed my heart wi' feelings fine, wi' noble thoughts
 my heid,
My latest breath shall melt away in blessings on
 the Tweed.

SHE'S SWEET, SHE'S FAIR

Air—"*She's fair an' fause.*"

She's sweet, she's fair, an' oh! she's dear,
How dear lips canna tell!
It's no for rank, it's no for gear,
I love the lass sae well.

But she is false as she is fair—
Yet wha can wi' the jaud compare?
There's something in my heart cries, where?
An' chills me like a knell.

I'd fain forget, but oh! that smile
Aye floats before my e'e;
Where'er I turn, yon dimpling wile
Will no let me gang free.
Like clouds that breathe in summer rain
New life to flowers on hill or plain,
She gae me life—but she's ta'en't again—
She's stown the peace from me.

OH! DOOL ON THE DAY I WAS MARRIED.

Air—"*Up in the Morning.*"

Oh! dool on the day, oh! dool on the day,
That day to the kirk I was hurried—
To wed Jenny Birse for better or warse,
I wish it had been to be buried.
She flytes i' the morn, she flytes i' the night,
Wi' flyting an' fighting I'm worried,
Tho' I were an angel I wadna be right,
Oh! dool on the day I was married.

She's queen o' the pantry, queen o' the kist,
A' things by her maun be ferry'd;
There's naething she misses that shouldna be
    miss'd,
Oh! dool on the day I was married.

The dog in its rancour trots bantering by,
Wi' tailie an' nosie high carried,
An' ventures a youf, in scorn o' the coof,
Oh! dool on the day I was married.

When neebors are near, why then I'm her dear,
An' Maister Balwhather is serried,
The best o' the dish, be't haggis or fish,
Yet dool on the day I was married.
The denner scarce dune, an' the neebors are gane,
How the tone o' her leddyship's varied!
You ne'er-do-weel chiel, gang hence to the de'il,
Oh! dool on the day I was married.

At the kirk she sits in the minister's seat,
Her leddyship there maun be carried,
While puir Cumdoddie maun trot on his feet,
Oh! dool on the day I was married.
A week but bygane, ere the sermon began,
Wi' her I'd been sae mickle flurried,
I sang in a qualm instead o' the psalm,
Oh! dool on the day I was married.

YE FATHERS.

Air—"*My Tocher's the Jewel.*"

YE fathers wha worship the penny siller;
Ye mothers wha heed no affection true,
Oh! think o' the days gane when ye were younkers,
When love it was trusting an' strong in you.

Remember ye no when ye first heard love's
    whisper,
Thought ye o' the warld's gear when first young
    love spak'?
Yet now when wi' you twa the sweet time is over,
The hearts ye have nurtured why ye wad break.

Oh! look on yon e'e, where the saut tear is starting,
Oh! look on the grey-beard wha sits by her side,
Wha only can brag o' his age an' his fortune,
An' yet ye wad doom her to be his sad bride.
Oh! saw ye the snaw ever cherish the fire?
Oh! saw ye the hawk ever pair wi' the doo?
The loud voice o' nature cries no, in its ire,
The beasts o' the forest are kinder than you.

WHAT AM I?

What am I that I should bow
To a decorated brow;
Or my face give forth to view,
What my heart feels is not true?
Be I right or be I wrong,
Be it ever on my tongue,
For no man shall say that I
E'er gave utt'rance to a lie.

Be he rich or be he poor,
He who entereth my door,
If he have of good his part,
He shall find an open heart;
But if he come in disguise,
False his lips and false his eyes;
If his acts his words deny,
I will tell him of the lie.

Whilst I live, oh! let me love,
All the truth that I can prove,
In my inmost sense it feel,
Tho' my very brain should reel;
Let it be to me as air,
Let me breathe it everywhere;
So no man shall say that I
E'er gave utt'rance to a lie.

MILLICENT MORAN.

Young Millicent Moran was married in May,
To Phelim who'd loved her for many a day;
But Phelim was kinless and Phelim was poor,
And Millicent's friends never darkened their door.
Yet oft as the tear-drop came up in her eye,
Poor Phelim would soothingly, smilingly cry,
"O Milly dear, Milly dear, bear this in mind,
There's wealth in the house, when our hearts are but kind."

The young as they passed her looked on her in scorn,
The old shook their grey heads, and from her did turn;
But time soon the bosom healed, pride had made sore,
Her grief grew the less as her love grew the more;
For oft as the tear-drop came up in her eye,
Poor Phelim would soothingly, smilingly cry,
"O Milly dear, Milly dear, bear this in mind,
There's wealth in the house when our hearts are but kind."

'Twas love, earnest love, that this rapid change
 wrought.
Poor Phelim he toiled, and he read, and he
 thought,
And little cared he for the scorn of the gay,
By honest industry grew wealthy as they :
No more comes the tear-drop in Millicent's eye,
The oft spoken words are the comforting cry,
" O Milly dear, Milly dear, bear this in mind,
There's wealth in the house when our hearts are
 but kind."

OH ! WHAT ARE FRIENDS?

Air—*The Dream.*

Oh! what are friends, the best, the nearest,
When false love the heart has torn ?
Robb'd o' a' that life holds dearest,
I maun live, an' I maun mourn.
To ilk thing has nature given
Kindred mate o' kindred hue ;
But to me has nature striven
To gie me who proved untrue.

On the bonnie blooming heather,
Bess an' I how oft we lay,
Sweet the kiss an' vow together,
Hopes o' joy beyond decay ;
Swore I by yon bright sun shining,
I'd be true an' I'd be kind,
Swore she too, but she designing,
Kept faith like the faithless wind.

NANNY.

AIR—"*Fee him Father.*"

THERE'S mony a flow'r beside the rose,
And sweets beside the honey;
But laws maun change ere life disclose
A flow'r or sweet like Nanny.
Her e'e is like the summer sun,
When clouds can no conceal it,
Ye're blind if it ye look upon,
Oh! mad if e'er ye feel it.

I've mony bonnie lasses seen,
Baith blythesome, kind an' canny;
But oh! the day has never been,
I've seen another Nanny;
She's like the Mavis in her sang,
Amang the breakans bloomin'
Her lips ope to an angel's tongue,
But kiss her, oh! she's woman.

I CANNA LIE.

AIR—"*The Blathrie o't.*"

I CANNA lie, I canna gang;
A weel faur'd lass has been my death,
She's stown my heart, she's stown my sang,
She's stown away my very breath.

Yet oh! but little kent she how
She gae to me that mortal wound:
As aye another glance she threw
An' aye there came another stound.

There's surely magic in the air
That floats around their honey mou's,
Although we ken the ruin there,
The ruin we can no refuse.

Like wee birds which the serpent wiles,
By charmed brightness o' its e'e,
When woman thraws on us her smiles,
We can but lay us doon an' dee.

MY BESSIE.

Air—*The Posie*.

My Bessie, oh! but look upon these bonnie budding flow'rs,
Oh! do they no remember ye o' mony happy hours,
When on this green and gentle hill we aften met to play,
An' ye were like the morning sun, an' life a nightless day?

The gowans blossomed bonnilie, I'd pu' them from the stem,
An' rin in noisy blythesomeness to thee, my Bess, wi' them,
To place them in thy lily breast, for ae sweet smile on me,
I saw nae mair the gowans then, then saw I only thee.

Like two fair roses on a tree, we flourished an' we grew,
An' as we grew, sweet love grew too, an' strong, 'tween me and you.
How aft ye'd twine your gentle arms in love about my neck,
An' breathe young vows that after years o' sorrow has no brak!

We'd raise our lisping voices in auld Coila's melting lays,
An' sing that tearfu' tale about Doon's bonnie banks and braes;
But thought na we o' banks an' braes, except those at our feet,
Like yon wee birds we sang our sang, yet ken'd no that 'twas sweet.

Oh! is na this a joyous day, a' Nature's breathing forth,
In gladness an' in loveliness owre a' the wide, wide earth?
The linties they are lilting love on ilka bush an' tree,
Oh! may such joy be ever felt, my Bess, by thee an' me.

AN AULD MAN'S SONG.

AIR—"*O' a' the airts the wind can blaw.*"

OH! lead me where the wild flow'rs grow,
The bonny heather bell;
Where Nature's buds in beauty blow,
An' scent baith moor an' dell.

AN AULD MAN'S SONG.

Oh! let me gaze before I die
On Tweedale's fairest lea,
Where ilka breeze in gentle sigh
Breathed love wi' you an' me.

Oh! let me see that sunny knowe,
We oft hae trod in youth,
Beneath the fragrant haw-tree bough,
We pledged our love an' troth.
When ilka tree was clad in green,
An' bloom o' varied hue,
Sweet smiles in every flow'r were seen,
There stown, my Bess, from you.

Oh! do ye mind that summer night,
When you and I were there?
Your e'en outshone the starry light,
My lips they breathed a prayer;
Ye told me what in whisper low
Nae longer ye could shun;
'Twa hearts embraced in happy glow,
Which love said were but one.

My Bess, ye were a gleesome quean
As ever owned a mind,
Few peers had you on hill or green,
Sae modest, sweet an' kind;
But flowers live to bloom an' die,
The shrub an' forest tree;
An' a' that owns an earthly tie
Maun fade like you an' me.

My eyes grow dim, and runneth slow
The purple stream at last,
An' life seems a dull vision now,
Or faint dream o' the past.
But there is still that promised land,
Where age is not, nor pain ;
Oh yes ! we'll join that happy band,
And sing o' days bygane.

DOCTOR O'SLEE.

Air—*Laird of Cockpen.*

Oh ! heard ye the like o't in countrie or toon ?
Oh ! saw ye the match o't in print written doon ?
A widow was won by the blink o' an e'e,
An' the saft-speaking tongue, o' Doctor O'Slee.

The widow's young daughter an heiress was born,
She'd gowpens o' siller an' stackfu's o' corn,
An' it clippit the tongue, an' it saftened the e'e,
O' Caverton's widow, wi' Doctor O'Slee.

The daughter's auld sire had been a braw laird,
Wi' Caverton farm an' Caverton yaird,
When she cam o' age to spend she was free—
I'll save her the trouble, thought Doctor O'Slee.

The daughter grew fair, an' the daughter grew tall,
She wanted to keek a wee ow're the auld wall ;
But she mauna gang out, nor she mauna gang see,
Except in the keeping o' Doctor O'Slee.

Wherever steps she, another maun trace,
Be it preaching or party, close veiled is her face,
" In love she shall no wi' a living thing be,
Not even the Gospel," said Doctor O'Slee.

" Gudewife, think no ye that our Maggie lies lang,
Maybe the vile toothache has gi'en her a stang?
Sae rin awa to her, my dawtie, an' see
Why tarries the lassie," said Doctor O'Slee.

The dawtie cam rinnin in fury and wae,
" To the toll wi' the tailor she's trampit away;"
" Pills, potions an' plaisters gang wi' her," roar'd he;
The shock drove the life out o' Doctor O'Slee.

THE WIND BLAWS CAULDLY.

AIR—"*He's owre the hills.*"

THE wind blaws cauldly through the door,
The ase lies moist on the hearth-stane,
An' bare's the wa', and bare's the floor,
Where I am left to mourn my lane.
Young Jamie's words were sweet an' fair,
My e'en were blind, owre blind for me,
For oh! was falsehood lurking there
Within the kiss he gae to me.

The ray that fa's on yonder flow'r,
The show'r that's life unto the tree,
Is no sae sweet as was that hour
He breathed a world o' care to me.

I see the bank where oft we lay,
I hear the vows he used to make;
But oh! like light they melt away,
An' leave my trusting heart to break.

The laverock sings on joyous wing,
An' blythesome sips the thrifty bee,
There's joy, for every living thing,
But joy, alas! there's nane for me.
It's hard to bear a lover's frown;
It's hard to part when we hae met,
When every pleasure's been our own—
But oh! it's harder to forget.

OH! MICKLE BEAUTY.

Air—*Roy's Wife*.

Oh! mickle beauty, Love, is thine,
Oh! mickle joy to me is given.
The blessed thought that ye'll be mine,
Makes me forget to think o' heaven.
As two young stems together cling,
We'll live ae life o' love an' gladness,
Around us no a breathing thing
Shall ever feel the pain o' sadness.

As dewy leaves on flow'r or tree
Greet aye the sun wi' smiles o' pleasure,
So shall I ever turn to thee,
Like ony miser to his treasure.
The rose o' love, sae cherry red,
Each clime can rear, nae blast can wither,
Deep planted in the heart an' head,
It blooms wi' life—they die together.

JEAN SITS ON YON HILLOCK.

AIR—"*Yellow-haired Laddie.*"

JEAN sits on yon hillock a' the lang day,
Singing "wae's me, my Jamie is now wede away,"
And aye as the burthen is borne in the air,
A sigh from her bosom cries echo is there.

Her Jamie lies buried under yon stane,
She watches his pillow, watches her lane;
His love was her feeling, his form was her pride,
She prized him abune a' the wide warld beside.

Wha sleeps sae serenely on yon cauld bed?
It's Jean sleeping soundly the sleep o' the dead;
She died sighing o'er him, she breathed her last lay,
"I'll sing to thee, Jamie, a' the lang day."

HOW SWEET TO HEAR.

AIR—"*There grows a bonnie briar bush.*"

HOW sweet to hear a melody o' our ain land!
How sweet to gie in charity wi' bounteous hand!
But o' a' the warld's joys the only ane for me
Is to prie a lassie's mou' when the love is in her e'e.

There dwells a bonnie lassie, oh! I ken where,
  She's kind an' oh! she's modest, and far better than fair;
They say she is na bonnie, but the false, false lips they lee,
They never pried her mou' when the love was in her e'e.

I've heard the warld prate oft o' beauty rare,
I've heard a coof relate o' a handsome shape an'
    air ;
But I heard na o' the ardent heart that beats sae
    kind for me,
When I prie my lassie's mou' when the love is in
    her e'e.

A CARLE CAM TO OUR HA' GATE.

Air—"*Auld wife ayont the fire.*"

A CARLE cam to our ha' gate,
Ae winter's night when unco late ;
The wind was strong an' driving sleet,
He prayed to let him in O !
" Oh ! weary, wet, an' cold am I,"
He spak wi' mony a heavy sigh,
" Sweet ladye, help or I maun die,
If ye no let me in O !
    Me in O ! me in O !
    If ye no let me in O !
Tho' mickle lack I warld's gear,
I wat it's no great sin O !"

Auld granny, honest, pious woman,
Was on her knees a prayer bummin',
But up she got when she heard comin'
Some carle to get in O !
" A bed, gudeman, we coudna' gie
E'en to a king, an' you were he ; "
Wee Jenny looked wi' kinder e'e,
She sleely let him in O !

Him in O! him in O!
She sleely let him in O!
"Creep canny up the stairs, puir carle,
An' mind ye mak nae din O!"

About the hour o' twal' that night,
Auld granny wakened in a fright,
Crying "surely," as she sat upright,
"I heard a lassie grane O!
I surely heard the lassie scream;"
"O granny dear, ye do but dream,
The rattens they were at the cream,
Oh! gang to sleep again O!
Again O! again O!
Oh! gang to sleep again O!
We'll get a trap the morn's morn,
And catch them every ane O!"

But granny she was frighten'd sair,
To Jenny's bed went up the stair;
Gude Lord! she found when she got there,
Mair in the bed than ane O!
Her e'en like lowing coals did shine,
"Ye limmer, leave this house o' mine."
"O granny dear, but read the 'line,'
The Priest did mak us ane O!
Us ane O! us ane O!
The Priest did mak us ane O!
It's Johnny Tait frae yont the gate,
Your blessing on us twain O!"

MY OLD WIFE.

My old wife has neither grace
In her form nor in her face;
Cherry lips nor beaming eyes,
For whose sake your lover sighs;
Yet ill-favour'd tho' she be,
Oh! my wife is kind to me.

It is idleness to seek
For the blossom on her cheek;
The red rose, if ever there,
Life has written o'er with care;
Yet ill-favour'd tho' she be,
Oh! my wife is kind to me.

In her mind small trace is seen,
That a teacher there has been;
And her words come forth at will,
Some for good, and some for ill;
Yet ill-favour'd tho' she be,
Oh! my wife is kind to me.

Yet I would not in her face,
E'en a brighter feature trace;
Yet I would not in her mind
To her smallest fault be blind;
For ill-favour'd tho' she be,
Oh! my wife is kind to me.

What were features worth to him
Filled with sorrow to the brim?

What a bosom white as snow
With an empty heart below?
If he could not sing with glee,
"Oh! my wife is kind to me."

But how falsely have I sung!
My old wife's both fair and young;
Rich in cheeks, in lips and eyes,
That the saints themselves might prize;
Yet these charms I cannot see,
For her kindliness to me.

THE BRAES O' TWEEDALE.

Air—*Gloomy Winter.*

My blessing on the bonny braes,
They bring up mony bygane days;
As morning brings its sunny rays,
The bonnie braes o' Tweedale O!
The heart may for a time forget
The land where it an' life first met;
But mem'ry like a sun that's set,
Has ris'n again on Tweedale O!
An' do they once again appear,
The joyous scenes o' youthfu' year?
I canna help this glad, glad tear,
The bonnie braes o' Tweedale O!

Now do we sae in gladness meet,
The flow'rs that blossom at my feet;
The very gowan seems to greet
The bonnie braes o' Tweedale O!

Again I bless the gentle things,
They are to me o' life the springs,
The air that sweeps owre my heart-strings,
The bonnie braes o' Tweedale O!
I see my father's house and ha',
The laughing wee things in a raw;
My mother looking thro' them a',
The bonnie braes o' Tweedale O!

In mony beauteous lands I've been,
I've gazed on mony a bonny scene;
But oh! 'mang a' that met my e'en,
I met nae braes o' Tweedale O!
The soul that dwells in mortal frame,
Ne'er yearned to heav'n wi' purer flame,
Than I to them, my ancient hame,
The bonnie braes o' Tweedale O!
As mother cleaves to her first-born,
So next my heart shall they be worn,
If I forget them may I mourn,
The bonny braes o' Tweedale O!

MY SWEET LASSIE.

Air—"*The waes o' Scotland.*"

[This Song is published by Jefferys & Co., Soho Square.]

Oh! but look on my sweet lassie,
Nae pearls to deck her head,
Stepping along thro' the gaudy throng,
Wi' light and gracefu' tread;
Nae jewels her's to tell o' wealth,
How fortune has been kind.
The dow'r o' my love, it lies in her health,
In her warm heart and mind.

Oh! but see her brow, my lassie's
Hung round wi' silken hair;
Sweet 'tis to kiss with a hungering mou'
The beauty dwelling near.
I lie me by her feet sae sma',
And sma' are they, I ween:
To feast on the thoughts that gracefully fa'
From her ripe lips and e'en.

Gang she west or east, my lassie,
Joy aye gangs her before;
Nought can be sadly wi' man, wife or beast,
When she's within the door.
There's nothing mean, there's nothing rude,
Can near my love be found,
Her face it reflecteth a' that is gude,
Upon the blessed ground.

WHY DO YE TARRY?

Why do ye tarry
Bonny ship Mary?
Why do ye linger, sae far, far frae me?
Winds will ye wauken,
Ne'er your breath slacken,
But oh! blow kindly, my love's on the sea.

If o' her nature
Ye had a feature,
Ne'er could ye harm the frail barque on the sea.
Not even find weather
To ruffle a feather
O' the puir sea bird, sae gentle is she.

But if ye'll not send
My dear love to land,
Oh! bear this kiss hence in swiftness with thee;
Say not unto her
Wha is the wooer,
She'll ken by the kiss, that the kiss comes from me.

THE LAD WHA'LL SOON BE FAR AWA'.

AIR—"*Gude night an' joy.*"

A' YE wha ever grasped the hand
O' friendship ardent and sincere,
Come drink wi' me, ye kindred band,
The health o' ane to friendship dear.
It's not by custom's rule we drink
To lord, or knave, or fool ava;
The heart to feel, the head to think,
The lad wha'll soon be far awa'.

We've seen the king upon his throne
To mony lands decrees impart;
His name engraved on wood and stone,
But writ not on a single heart.
Whene'er we find in human kind
The man in thought, in deed, in a',
We'll hail a king in heart and mind,
The lad wha'll soon be far awa'.

The green, green leaves that yonder hang,
Must part forthwith at winter's ca';
E'en sae must we, howe'er the pang,
From him wha'll soon be far awa'.

Oh! may our wishes be the wind,
That wafts him to his distant ha';
And may he think o' those behind,
The lad wha'll soon be far awa'.

MENIE HAY.

AIR—"*Heigh-ho! for somebody.*"

A WEE bird sits upon a spray,
And aye it sings o' Menie Hay,
The burthen o' its cheerie lay,
Is "Come away, dear Menie Hay.
Sweet art thou, O Menie Hay;
Fair, I trow, O Menie Hay;
There's not a bonny flow'r in May,
Shows a bloom wi' Menie Hay."

A light in yonder window's seen,
And wi' it seen is Menie Hay;
Wha gazes on the dewy green,
Where sits the bird upon the spray?
"Sweet art thou, O Menie Hay;
Fair, I trow, O Menie Hay;
At sic a time, in sic a way,
What seek ye there, O Menie Hay?"

"What seek ye there, my daughter dear?
What seek ye there, O Menie Hay?"
"Dear mother, but the stars sae clear
Around the bonnie milky way."
"Sweet art thou, O Menie Hay;
Slee, I trow, O Menie Hay;
Ye something see, ye daurna say,
Paukie, winsome Menie Hay."

The window's shut, the light is gane
And wi' it gane is Menie Hay;
But wha is seen upon the green,
Kissing sweetly Menie Hay?
"Sweet art thou, O Menie Hay;
Slee, I trow, O Menie Hay;
For ane sae young ye ken the way,
And far from blate, O Menie Hay."

"Gae scour the country, hill and dale;
Oh! waes me, where is Menie Hay?
Search ilka nook, in town or vale,
For my daughter, Menie Hay."
"Sweet art thou, O Menie Hay;
Slee I trow, O Menie Hay;
I wish ye joy, young Johnny Fay,
O' your bride, sweet Menie Hay."

FAREWELL TO THE LAND.

Air—"*Kitty Tyrell.*"

Farewell to the land of our fathers, farewell!
A land once as free as its waters that flow;
The slaves of a tyrant have sounded thy knell,
The despot has triumphed and Poland lies low.

Oh! shades of our fathers in pity look o'er us,
What once was your home, now's a mouldering pile;
The land that ye loved lies in ashes before us,
And Poland's but heard in the voice of exile.

No more shall your daughters e'er cherish a smile,
To greet the returning of hearts that are dear;
No more shall their lips e'er our sorrows beguile,
Bright eyes that once beamed, now are dimm'd with a tear.

Those strains now are heard not that told of your might,
Which fame has borne far over mountain and wave;
No more will love's voice ever swell with delight,
But sink into sighs o'er the tombs of the brave.

No home for the exile, no refuge from danger,
No laws but the laws which a despot has made;
Yet some lips will pray for the wandering stranger,
And hearts they will feel, and their hands proffer aid.

I'VE LOVED THEE.

I'VE loved thee, Love, long; I've loved thee, Love, deep;
I love thee awake, Love; I love thee asleep;
While I think, while I feel, while I smile, while I weep,
  By day, and by night, and in dream.
Though never by me have your praises been sung,
Tho' ne'er have I said you were charming and young;
You dwell in my heart, Love, and not on my tongue,
  And there are you dweller supreme.

The earth never boasts of the depth of its hoards;
The air never tells of the life it affords;
The sun gives its light, yet it utters no words—
   Now surely you'll own they are true.
My eyes cannot look, Love; my lips cannot tell
The tide of my heart, in its ebb, or its swell;
I cannot let others see how I love well!
   Yet still do I worship but you.

WATTY'S WEDDING.

Air—"*Green grow the rushes O!*"

There ne'er was seen sic sport and play,
At either kirk or bedding O!
As so fell out upon a day,
At rhyming Watty's wedding O!
Oh! for Watty's wedding O!
Hey for Watty's wedding O!
The de'il that day he took the play,
To dance at Watty's wedding O!

The bride she waited at the kirk
Twa lang, lang hours for Watty O!
An' when he cam' she ca'd him stirk,
An' gae his pow a clawtie O!
Oh! for Watty's wedding O!
   &c., &c., &c.

He glow'red an' trembled like a leaf,
An' tried to calm his dawtie O!
She stapped his mou' wi' double nief,
A crimson neb gat Watty O!
Oh! for Watty's wedding O!
   &c., &c., &c.

She ca'd him gowk, she ca'd him rogue,
Did Watty's darling dawtie O !
But whether he was man or dog,
The fient a bit kent Watty O !
Oh ! for Watty's wedding O !
    &c., &c., &c.

Some leugh aside, some pity cried,
Some ran away retreating O !
The priest looked up to Heaven an' sighed,
The bridegroom fell a greeting O !
Oh ! for Watty's wedding O !
    &c., &c., &c.

But now he's tethered by a string,
An' curses the mischancie O !
That set him wooing sic a dame,
Sae vile a jaud as Nancy O !
Oh ! for Watty's wedding O !
    &c., &c., &c.

ELIZA.

AIR—" *O Jean, I love thee.*"

OH ! fragrant ever be the dell,
Where first Eliza smiled on me :
Nae earthly tongue can ever tell
Her beauty under that May tree ;
The woods threw off their wintry gloom,
An' gladness filled the scented air ;
Auld Eve hersel' in Eden's bloom,
Was ne'er to Adam half sae fair.

Upon her brow are graces rare ;
Her e'en like suns speak out in light ;
Their gentlest glance will utter mair
Than ever mortal pen could write ;
Within her lips such feelings lie,
They melt me as in words they flow ;
Were she to bid me gang an' die,
I coudna for my life say no.

When she's in heaven, where a' is fair
An' gude beyond our human ken ;
Where virtues grow they say so rare,
She cannot look more lovely then.
O Death ! however sure thy dart,
In morning life, in life's decay,
Pray tell me could ye hae the heart
To steal such loveliness away.

IF THERE WERE FEELING.

AIR—"*Johnny's grey breeks.*"

IF there were feeling in the air,
An' it could taste o' dear delight,
Its life for my love I wad bear,
An' be her breath baith day an' night.
Her bosom I wad make my throne,
Her throbbing heart be ever nigh ;
An' speak its joys in kindred tone,
Yet never mix'd wi' ae sad sigh.

I'd bear to her the richest scent
That ever came frae out the ground ;
Sweet songs my love should never want,
The sweetest ever told in sound.

I'd play amang her hair that mocks
The finest threads e'er nature framed ;
The gracefu' waving o' her locks
Should make the very trees ashamed.

Her guardian wad I be from wrong
While sleep amang her senses crept ;
Tho' lightning prayed for thunder's tongue
I wadna whisper while she slept.
How sweet within her cells to rest !
While she respired me at her ease ;
I'd never leave her heaving breast,
Tho' death should beg upon his knees.

ONE EVENING.

AIR—"*Tak' your auld cloak about ye.*"

One evening, in the bright moonlight,
I musing sat upon a stile ;
Twa voices brak' the silent night,
Which made my fancy pause awhile.
I heard an angry, angry wife,
On her gudeman her tongue let flee ;
"Oh ! I wad lead an angel's life,
If I frae my gudeman were free."

The husband was a patient carle,
But Lucky's tongue brought up his ire ;
It galloped on in sic a whirl—
Had there been snow 'twad been on fire
"If ye'd been Eve, the ancient fool
Had surely ne'er been led by thee ;
As you dislike the wedded rule,
Gae hang yersel' ; then ye'll be free."

I wandered on, an' as I went,
I thought how silly mortals stray
From Nature's laws, her kind intent,
While wooing for a marriage day.
If men wad think before they wed
That like wi' like can but agree,
'Twad save the heart, as aft the head,
An' wives wad always angels be.

YE BONNY SUN.

AIR—"*O' a' the airts the wind can blaw.*"

Oh! shine away, ye bonny sun,
Ye look a blythesome thing;
Wi' you how mony ills we shun!
How mony joys ye bring!
There's no a flow'r in a' the vale;
There's naething ever grew,
Nor heart but your kind blessings feel;
And, feeling, blesses you.

Oh! shine away, ye bonny thing,
A' nature's blooming fair;
The new mawn fields their odours fling
Along the balmy air.
The trees hae on their richest green,
True love lies in the shade;
What gladness fills the happy scene
The gladness ye hae made.

I love my Jean, my ain gudewife,
I love my bairnies too;
Each day ye bring them joys to life,
And aye ilk joy is new.

There's joy in yonder clear blue sky;
There's joy on yonder sea:
The very air is singing joy,
In echoes back to me.

I love to see your parting smile,
As ye set in the west;
To rise on mony distant isle,
And rising make them blest.
Oh! may I in my setting hour,
Be calm as your adieu!
And live again like thee in pow'r,
As bright and blessing too.

WHEN SUMMER DAYS.

Air—"*Willie brew'd a peck o' maut.*"

When summer days were in their prime,
And nature lookit glad and fair,
Three chiels forgathered on a time,
To breathe a wee the cauler air.
They wandered east, they wandered west,
And aye they sang amang the fields;
The burthen o' their song was "blest,
Are a' the joys that nature yields!"

Kind Richard, wi' the gentle e'en,
And Wully, wi' the forehead hie;
Twa likely lads as e'er were seen,
And rhyming Sandy made the three;
They wandered east, they wandered west,
&c., &c., &c.

They saw a bonny budding rose,
New sprung from out its parent earth;
Cried Richard, "That sweet flower shows
An emblem o' our infant birth."
They wandered east, they wandered west,
&c., &c., &c.

They next cam' to a branchless tree,
The worm was eating fast away;
Said Wully, "In that trunk you see
An emblem o' life's sad decay."
They wandered east, they wandered west,
&c., &c , &c.

But here three lasses owre the hill
Right fairy-like cam' tripping doon;
Roar'd Sandy, "Preach away your fill,
Behold the flow'rs o' heav'n aboon!"

A MINSTREL.

A MINSTREL sang in a garden bower,
To a maiden fair and sweet;
As a smile that speaks in the love-lit hour,
When love's eyes, love's eyes meet:
The maiden look'd like a beauteous flower
In the blooming month of May;
The minstrel sang with bewitching power,
   "Sweet maiden, come away,
      Oh! come away; yes, come away,
      Come, come away."

"The lark, he sings of his love on high,
While his fond mate lists below
To each sweet note from the clear blue sky,
With a lover's ardent glow.
The buds, like joys in the youthful breast,
Burst forth on flow'r an' tree;
But what are they to me, unbless'd,
Without love's smile from thee?
  Oh! come away; yes, come away,
  Come, come away."

The maiden look'd; she a rose espied,
To another it bent its head;
Which blushed as deep as a new-made bride,
O'er whom love's power is shed.
Two linnets wooing, her quick eye caught,
As they warbled on a spray;
She felt 'twas love, and she paused and thought.
The minstrel sang, "Away,
  Oh! come away; yes, come away,
  Come, come away."

She looked again; but no rose was there,
And the linnets they were gone;
No minstrel's music filled the air;
Did the maiden stay alone?
Ah! no, she had fled far over the vale,
Close press'd to her lover's side;
The sweet-tongued minstrel of Teviotdale
Had won her for his bride.
  She fled away like a sunny ray,
  In the month of May.

SONGS.

MY WIFIE WEE.

Air—"*Aye wakin O!*"

My wifie wee;
Sulky oft, oft cheerly;
Tho' she taks the gee;
Yet still I love her dearly,
    My wifie wee.

She has an ill-faur'd tongue,
I never saw the lave o't;
I've aften said and sung,
Oh! could I see the grave o t.
    My wifie wee;
    &c., &c., &c.

Whatever drink be brew'n,
She maun see the brewing;
Whatever maun be dune,
She maun hae the doing.
    My wifie wee;
    &c., &c., &c.

Howe'er her humours range,
Howe'er her tongue gangs clatter;
Yet I wadna change,
I might na get a better.
    My wifie wee;
    &c., &c., &c.

JESSY RAE.

Air—"*Bonnie Mary Hay.*"

Bonnie Jessy Rae, wi' mind love has birth,
It's like the free air on the land or the sea ;
It's born in the heavens, it grows on the earth,
Wi' you it is life, ye are dear life to me.

Bonnie Jessy Rae, they may chain an angry tongue,
But they canna chain love's voice, it speaks in the e'e ;
The lips may be silent, the sang be no sung,
But oh! love will speak if it only can see.

Bonnie Jessy Rae, ye hae sworn to be mine,
To you I'll be true as the saut to the sea ;
The vows we hae taken, we ne'er will resign,
While our minds live in light, when they do no we'll dee.

CAN I FORGET?

Air—"*My friend and pitcher.*"

Can I forget what once I've seen,
In Teviot dale, on Teviot river ?
Can I forget what once I've been ?
Sweet, sweet remembrance, asks me—ever ?
My Bessie haunts me like a ghaist,
Her lips in fancy oft I pree them ;
Lips only fit for gods to taste,
Her e'en the light for gods to see them.

Oh! warld, ye may be ever night,
I care na tho' ye ne'er bring morrow;
Tho' ye be dark, yet I'll be light,
And far above your deepest sorrow;
For mem'ry warms my throbbing heart,
In it I see that sweet wee lassie,
'Twill be to me o' life a part;
'Twill be to me my bonnie Bessie.

A HEALTH TO HIM WHO THINKS.

Air—"*A man's a man for a' that.*"

While princes rule by whip and steel,
Are we to bend the knee,
When heaven gave us pow'r to feel
That we were born as free?
Shall freemen, like poor slaves, be wrought
To fear oppression's links?
In bumpers let us drink in thought,
A health to him who thinks.

Though tyrants bind us round and round
With chains in dungeon fast,
Our minds can ne'er in chains be bound
While reason's strength shall last.
We'll tell it to the dungeon walls;
We'll breathe it through its chinks:
Good men shall drink in good men's halls,
A health to him who thinks.

Great nature craves that men should think,
Each one in his degree,
For thinkers ne'er a nation sink,
They keep a people free.

There's not a bird on tree or wing
That of sweet music drinks,
But seems instinctively to sing
The health of him who thinks.

A COTTER I.

A COTTER I, wha ne'er deny
That I a cotter live, man,
A brother's sorrow never fly,
Ne'er take when I can give, man
Though scant o' meat an' claes, man,
Mid poverty an' waes, man,
      Oh ! never shall
      My spirit fall,
While I my hand can raise, man.

A cotter you, to friendship true,
To hame an' bairnies sweet, man ;
A weel-worn coat prevents na you
From walking on your feet, man.
Tho' puir, yet are we proud, man,
An' dare to sing aloud, man,
      That men have shone
      By heart alone,
The want o't is the cloud, man.

Behold yon ducal son of strife,
Whase foot's on fortune's ba', man,
Wha lives on mony a thousand life,
An' glories in it a', man.

Wad we no rather be, man,
Puir men, an' feel we're free, man,
　　Than draw our breath
　　From blood an' death?
The kind men bear the gree, man.

MY BONNIE WEE NANNY.

AIR—"*Come under my Plaidie.*"

My bonnie wee Nanny, my blessings be on ye,
How oft hae I wished for a moment sae dear!
An' do ye thus press me, an' kiss me, an' bless me;
I'm dizzy wi' joy that I canna weel bear.
Your father's relentit, he'll never repent it,
My blessings on him be, as well as my dear.
Oh! I maun be dreaming; those modest eyes beaming,
How bright are the e'en that beam through a glad tear!

There's joy in the greeting o' love when love meeting,
That words half its sweetness can never reveal;
Looks breathe it in blisses, lips speak it in kisses,
To a' but love's sel wad love ever conceal.
And when in its power, how sweet is the hour,
When heart pledges heart, let come woe, let come weal!
My ain it is panting, wi' rapture enchanting,
Love's felt no till sorrow has proven it leal.

Should bairnies e'er bless us, wee Nannies caress us,
An' grow up in beauty an' character fair,
Oh! may we blast never their love, but cheer't ever,
Heaven ne'er made affection to sell like a ware.
When auld age comes stealing, our grey hairs revealing,
An' thinkings an' feelings begin to decay,
We'll think o' the beaming, the love that is gleaming
Between us, dear Nanny, on this happy day.

TO MY WIFE.

AIR—"*Pinkey House.*"

[Written on the occasion of the Queen's visiting the City, on Lord Mayor's Day, 1837.]

We'll not go nigh the sight to-day
For pomp or fashion's sake,
But have at home a holiday,
That we ourselves shall make.
Thou'lt be a queen of love to me,
My heart shall be thy throne;
Lips, ears, and eyes thy subjects be,
And loyal every one.

We'll gaze upon our blood and kind,
That in the cradle lies,
And learn together from the mind,
New wak'ning in her eyes.

We'll see our forms and features mix'd,
In less or more degree;
What earthly scene can come betwixt
That sight and you and me?

The world from pomp can pleasure buy,
Oft for it dearly pay,
Yet is it only of the eye,
And dieth with the day.
When life from mutual love is drawn,
Life knows no setting sun,
But while we talk, behold the dawn—
Our holiday's begun.

THERE'S JOY NAE MAIR IN ANNIE'S E'E.

AIR—"*Jock o' Hazledean.*"

THERE'S joy nae mair in Annie's e'e,
Her joy is turned to sorrow:
Will Jamie never come from sea;
Will't never turn to-morrow?
The hand of time but slowly turns,
Another bends the knee;
She looks at him, but him she spurns,
For Jamie on the sea.

They've spread for her a bridal bed,
O' down is made the pillow,
An' to the kirk they'd hae her led:
She'd rather seek the willow,
The leaf unto the show'r is true;
The sap unto the tree:
Her heart, O Jamie, beats for you;
Her heart is on the sea.

A barque upon the wave is seen,
Anon it greets the shore;
Two lovers meet upon the green,
Who meet to part no more.
An' glad are they no more to part,
The tear speaks in their e'e,
For Jamie he had aye her heart,
Her heart has left the sea.

MY JEANNIE.

Oh! fa', fa', ye showers,
　　Awaken the flowers,
An' press their dry lips wi' your diamonds o' dew;
　　Nae mair be they wearie,
　　But laughing an' cheerie,
Each bud kiss its love, an' while kissing bless you.
　　Oh! flowers be springing,
　　Wee birdies be singing,
Look joyously a', for my Jeannie is true.

　　They told me that slighted
　　My love was, an' blighted
The hopes that but lived in the light o' her e'e;
　　Does earth slight the sunbeam,
　　Or ocean the moon-gleam,
As soon wad they slight, as my Jeannie slight me.
　　Oh! flowers be springing,
　　Wee birdies be singing,
Sweet smiles burst like blossoms on ilka green tree.

Her heart it was sleeping,
　　　Her e'en they were peeping
On forms than Robin's mair pridefu' than fair;
　　　Awakened to feeling,
　　　Her heart then revealing,
Through her blue e'en stealing, told Robin dwelt
　　there.
　　　　Oh! flowers be springing,
　　　　Wee birdies be singing,
Ye fields an' ye forests nae mair seem ye bare.

　　　It is no the nation,
　　　It is no the station
That fans to affection the glow of the heart;
　　　There's something that's given
　　　To light it from heaven,
'Tis thought true love's feelings alone can impart.
　　　　Oh! flowers be springing,
　　　　Wee birdies be singing,
My Jeannie is true: where, now, world's your
　　dart?

JOCK'S WIFE.

AIR—"*Weel may the keel row.*"

WHAT din is that in yon house?
Wha sings sae canty an' sae crouse,
As he o' life had found the use,
　　An' screwed a merry pin, O?
Oh! it is Jock, my brother Jock,
Whose sleep has been sae sairly broke.
He's ta'en a wife like ither folk,
　　To keep him up behin', O.

What din is that in yon house,
That breaks the rest o' neebors douce,
As a' the deils below were loose,
    An' kicking up a din, O ?
Oh ! it is Jean, my brother's wife,
Wha's breeding a' this raukle strife ;
She's clawed his pow an' sworn his life.
    He's been obliged to rin, O.

Jock's wife has ta'en a drapakie
Sae strang, the hizzie e'en maun dee ;
He's buried her wi' tearfu' e'e,
    But mickle joy within, O.
He's put a crape upon his hat,
An' noo he sleeps like ony cat.
He's ta'en an aith 'twill be his fau't
    If he weds wife again, O.

THE BARD.

It was upon a winter's day,
When heavy lay the snaw,
A bonnie birdie's waesome lay
Upon my ear did fa'.
"Oh ! gentle sir, I pray ye gang,
I pray ye gang wi' me."
Thus aye the bonnie birdie sang
In mournfu' melodie.

We cam unto a high, high hill,
Where wintry winds did blaw,
And there lay dead, sae calmly still,
A man amang the snaw.

My bonnie birdie, wha was he?
Had he nae kith nor kin?
Oh! still's the head, and dim's the e'e,
And cold the heart within.

The birdie to the body clung,
An' sang in accents dire,
" The sweetest bard that ever sung,
That ever struck the lyre.
But yesterday he sat wi' kings,
Their pleasure waited he;
But when his hand had left the strings,
They left him here to dee.

" He had the manliest, sweetest voice,
The darkest, brightest e'e;
He made the very birds rejoice,
Wi' his true harmonie.
On ilka thing he looked sae kind,
The smallest shrub or tree,
An' ca'd them part o' heart an' mind,
Yet hearts have let him dee."

I dug a grave upon the hill,
A grave below the snaw,
And laid the bard, sae cold and still,
Within his narrow ha'.
I had the blessing o' the bird,
His spirit from the air,
I blessed the bird that loved the bard,
Cursed those who left him there.

WHEN FLOWERS.

Air—"My only Jo and dearie O!"

When flowers were in their fairest bloom,
And perfume scented a' the air,
The linties sang amang the broom,
Oh! mickle joy had I to fear.
A lassie dwelt, weel ken I where,
Within a bonnie ocean town,
She had a look sae sweetly dear,
'Twad made a priest forget his gown.

She owned nae rank, and little gear,
Her heart was a' her penny fee;
A step sae light and skin sae fair,
Mair gracefu' than yon waving tree.
And though another had my love,
Yet still I pried that lassie's mou';
What tho' the sun shines bright above?
The moon and stars shine brightly too.

KING MIND.

A health unto the king
Who joins his cup to mine;
A health round let us sing,
Unto a king divine.
A king without a slave;
A chief chains cannot bind;
Nor mortals give a grave,
A health unto King Mind!

No king is he of pride,
He walks in homely guise;
Great worlds see deep and wide,
By radiance of his eyes.
His voice breathes budding spring
To all of human kind;
To every living thing,
A health to mighty mind.

I'VE WANDERED ON THE SUNNY HILL

I'VE wandered on the sunny hill, I've wandered in the vale,
Where sweet wee birds in fondness meet to breathe their am'rous tale;
But hills or vales, or sweet wee birds, nae pleasure's gae to me,
The light that beamed its rays on me was love's sweet glance from thee.

The rising sun in golden beams dispels the night's dark gloom,
The morning dew to roses' hue imparts a fresh'ning bloom;
But sunbeams ne'er sae brightly played in dance o'er yon glad sea,
Nor roses laved in dew sae sweet as love's sweet glance from thee.

I loved thee as the pilgrims love the water in the sand,
When scorching rays, or blue simoon, sweep o'er their with'ring hand;

The captive's heart nae gladlier beats, when set
    from prison free,
Than I when bound wi' beauty's chain, in love's
    sweet glance from thee.

I loved thee, bonnie Bessie, as the earth adores the
    sun,
I asked nae lands, I craved na gear, I prized but
    thee alone ;
Ye smiled in look, but no in heart—your heart was
    no for me ;
Ye planted hope that never bloomed in love's sweet
    glance from thee.

MY MOUNTAIN HAME.

Air—"*Galla Water.*"

My mountain hame! my mountain hame!
My kind, my independent mother;
While thought and feeling rule my frame,
Can I forget the mountain heather?
                  Scotland dear!

I love to hear your daughters dear,
The simple tale in sang revealing;
Whene'er your music greets my ear,
My bosom swells wi' joyous feeling,
                  Scotland dear!

Though I to other lands may gae,
Should fortune's smile attend me thither,
I'll hameward come, whene'er I may,
And look again on the mountain heather,
                  Scotland dear!

When I maun die, oh! I wad lie,
Where life and me first met together,
That my cold clay, through its decay,
Might bloom again in the mountain heather,
                              Scotland dear!

END OF SONGS.

POEMS.

INTRODUCTION TO A POEM.

When Summer shed its beauty o'er the land,
And circumstances smiled on me the while,
Often accompanied by a gentle friend—
Not friend in name, but in the word's best sense,
Bent I my footsteps tow'rds the country.
And it is sweet to minds worn down with cares
That business ever brings, to have one day
From out a number, that we can rise on
And bless as ours; whereon we may walk forth
With some we love, by those dear ones beloved,
And converse hold with the Eternal Spirit,
That teaches man (if he have aptitude
And will to learn) its laws which never change;
But work in love, through each created thing.

We made our paths where open fields were clad
With verdure, and the air with fragrance full,
And heard the thrifty bee send forth its song,
And saw it sip the honey from the flowers,
Whose modest heads peep out among the grass,
And seem content if they can only catch

A gentle portion of the passing shower,
Or some stray glances of the summer sun.
We wandered where the trees their branches waved
In full luxuriance of a summer's dress ;
And stood as if they guarded those frail plants
That nestle in the bosom of the earth,
And find it death to meet an angry wind.
Now would we climb the hills and look around
On many a mile of valley far below,
That lay close studded o'er with nature's gear,
Like some rich table in profusion spread,
Sufficient to bewilder sense, howe'er
Intent the eater's appetite ; there see
The corn fast rip'ning, waving to such time,
In such sweet harmony from side to side,
That every field seemed but a single reed
Attuned to music by the summer breeze.

Here would a mansion greet our eyes, well girt
With wood, and water, lawns, and gardens rich
In fruits and plants of various climes, on which
We'd have some speech ; its beauty, prospect far
And wide ; its value, too, would we scan o'er,
And say, assumingly, its owner thrived.
There would a cot peep out from some lone nook—
A humble structure of rude stones and thatch—
Yet clean and neat. Mayhap the poor abode
Of some kind heart that held its neighbour dear,
And nursed a feeling for another's weal,
The mighty magnetism of noble men,
That tells who are akin.
      As we went on
Some object interesting, new or strange,

Would ever greet us, and bring up such thoughts
As we had not before, yet worth a place
In our remembrance—the familiar things
That we had known since first we knew ourselves—
Whether the tenant of the wood or field,
A chirping sparrow or a daisy wild ;
Still were they welcome, and fresh pleasure sprang
From our new greetings ; for we were friends
A long time parted : and ran musing o'er
The old communings of our early years,
So drew the friendship closer than before.
There's not a form howe'er minute or mean,
That lives beneath or on the earth, but is
Of Nature's alphabet a letter, these it
Behoveth all to know ; or, who shall learn
From her clear book her great and glorious truths,
And learning, teach, when like an unschooled child,
He knows not e'en the letters that make up
His teacher's language ? even an insect,
The meanest thing that crawls, and most despised,
Has some dear history, which, when mastered—
Its station, power, means, and final end—
Must make the inquirer spare the spurned thing,
And bring him nearer God : the wish to know
Was more to us than food, or garb, or gold,
At least we thought so in our reasoning ;
And though the expression of our inward minds
Was often met with smiles and biting words,
Yet did we pass them by and wander on.

E'en thus we spent our time ; the blessed sun
Ne'er rose upon a day which we named ours,
And did not greet us on some green hill side ;

Nor ever came the night that lips could say
After the passing of those musing hours,
That we had learn'd aught useless in our walk,
Or reached our humble homes less worthy men.

One beauteous morning, I with my dear friend,
My "gentle Richard," (his kind qualities
Of head and heart had drawn this name from
 me,)
Strolled on for many a long and pleasant mile,
By hill and valley, through both wood and brake,
Close reading as we went, and storing up
Such thoughts and fancies as each object gave,
Deep in our mem'ries, when our wearied limbs
Began to hint that we had travelled far.
A cottage stood some roods from the road side,
Tow'rds which we bent our steps; an ancient
 tree
That looked as it had braved the storms and
 blasts
Of many winters, at each corner stood;
High their branches reared and closely met,
As if the four were parts of one great trunk;
Sweet plants crept o'er the wholesome white-
 washed front,
And gave their pleasant odours to the air;
Before the door, surrounded by a hedge,
There was a garden—limited 'tis true;
And common were the flowers that blossomed
 there,
But yet enough for all the owner's wants,
As every plant within it was to him
Like some dear child, whom he had nursed and
 reared
Even from its birth, whose history he knew,

And would run o'er, for very love's sweet sake,
As fluently as some fond mother tells
The fancied virtues of a favourite son,
And pleased was he to find at any time
Their simple beauty catch some passer's eye,
And make him linger on his way, to gaze.

Upon a seat of turf, reposing lay
The worthy owner of this rustic spot,
A man who seemed coeval with the trees,
Beneath whose branches he reclined at length.
He was on some old manuscript intent,
As if he read because he loved to know,
And reason on his knowledge ; not as one
Who turns a leaf to pass an idle hour,
And half in dulness, half in slumber sunk,
Lets go the hours, and all his reading too,
Without a shadow of a thought behind.
He rose as we approached, and on our wants
Being told to him, politely ushered us
Into the house—it wore a face of thrift,
And told in look, as plain as look could speak,
That slothfulness held not a lodgment there.
Upon an unclothed table, clean and white,
A plain repast was spread by his old dame,
Of milk yet warm, and bread that had been made
By her own hands, the sweetest meal that e'er
Was made my friend and I made there and then.
We found our host a man who had well trained
His thoughts and feelings, not by maxims preached,
Or rules laid down in books ; but what he saw
Among his fellows in an humble sphere

He hoarded up for profit; shrewd and kind,
He seemed as one who had gone through his
 time,
An old "John Anderson;" his wife fit mate
For such a "Jo," the very pair that Burns
Had drawn so true in his immortal song.

The dame was full of spirit as a child
That has not stumbled on its first sad thought:
Her ancient tongue ran on in gibe and jeer,
And wit rough hewn, tho' pointed, from her lips
Fell often heavily on the old man's head;
But he, kind heart, passed all in merry vein,
And took in love what had in love been sent;
Though in the middle of an argument
Would he break off the question unresolved,
And turn him round, with "fie, Old Folly, fie,
One foot within the grave, and still a fool,"
Addressed to her, half serious, half in jest,
Then laugh as heartily and loud as she.
'Twas beautiful to see the aged pair,
After an union of some fifty years,
Still young in all affection gives or craves;
The kind exchange of office and of speech—
The electricity of look, and tone—
The thousand things that lack both name and
 voice,
Yet bind all hearts well stored and well attuned
In general points, howe'er they differ in
A few details, were present and as fresh,
With seventy winters furrowed on their brows,
As it had been with them but summer youth,
The spring time of their marriage, and its joys.
Oh! ye who every morning rise the lords
Of millions, who by wealth and station seek,

Through all the paths of brief enduring sense,
A happy hour, and seek for it in vain ;
If ye have power to cast an honest look,
A wish to gather hope for after change,
Take note of such a pair, and learn that life
Is often best engaged apart from wealth,
Even below an humble cottage roof,
When hearts are all the coffers that are stored,
Looks, smiles, and kindly words the current coin
That from the mint come shining forth at will,
And not one counterfeit in all the heap.

Our host was full of ballads and old songs
That he had in his youthful days stored up,
For he was from the north, where runs the Tweed
With many a song and ballad intermixed :
" Gude Wallace," " Hughie Graham," " Etin Hynde,"
True " Lizzy Baillie," who in secret left
Her father's arms for those she worshipped more,
And was content to live in mean degree,
And drudge for him she loved ; the mermaid fair
Of Gallaway, and false as fair, who as

> " It fell in about the sweet summer month,
> I' the first come o' the mune,
> She sat o' the top o' a sea-weed rock,
> A kaming her silk locks down."

And many others, beautiful and true,
He chaunted o'er, and not more pleased was he
To tell his tale than we to sit and hear.
His mother was the source of all his song,
Of whom, with moistened eyes, he often told
Some early story newly summoned up,

Among a number of remembrances.

"Oft have we children sat upon her lap,
A-cold, with hunger gnawing at our hearts,
And lacking aught to stay the craving there :
To steal upon the time, and pain, would she,
Though care and sickness weighed her spirit down,
Recite wild legends of the English wars,
Or sing sweet songs of her dear native land.
We felt no more the cold or hunger then."

In such a strain he of his mother spoke,
The man of seventy years, yet then not old,
How she had reared him and a sister child,
Amid the pangs of poverty and want,
Related he the whole, and in such terms,
Such earnest heartiness of look and voice,
That e'en the tears came trickling from our eyes
In common sympathy with his discourse,
And we were ready to exclaim, oh! why
Should good men e'er grow old or die.
Old Time had galloped fast ; in truth were we
As much at home as at our own fire-side,
With all the family faces smiling round.
The eight-day clock that in the nook had stood
And ticked, and struck, for many a happy year,
Gave out the hour of ten—a hint to us
That fifteen weary miles lay dark and still
Between us and our homes. We rose and wished
Our friends good night, and thanks for their kind
    cheer ;
But, ere we reached the door, came tripping in
Our host's grand-daughter, a poor orphan girl,
Who lived with him, and that day had been
To meet a friend. She was the old man's joy,

And sung to him, when winter nights were long,
And few the comers to the rustic hearth,
The songs that took him back to other days,
When life itself was but an ancient song,
  A rude commingling of sweet thoughts and sounds;
And thus diffused through seventy mortal years
The healthy gladness of a mountain boy.

The old man wished our stay for some brief time,
That we might hear the orphan maiden sing.
We sate us down, not much against our will,
For we'd as soon have sat till that day week,
Or that day month, or year, or any time,
We loved so much to look upon the scene
That lay within those humble cottage walls.
" I prithee sing to us that ancient song
(The old man thus addressed the rustic maid)
That tells of Scotland, and of Scotland's hills.
'Twas coined by some sweet bard who died unknown,
But I do worship; and my simple brain
Drinks deep of childhood in the listening.
As some faint traveller on the arid sand
Alighted at the long, long looked for spring,
Gulps down the water through his parched lips
And drinks so sweetly, prays to thirst again
Whene'er Old Time shall cry, my hour is up,
I'd like to die to that same ancient song.
I prithee sing that song." The maid began.

SONG.

Oh! years hae come, an' years hae gane,
Sin' first I sought the warld alane!

Sin' first I mused wi' heart sae fain,
    On the hills o' Caledonia.
But oh! behold the present gloom,
My early friends are in the tomb,
An' nourish now the heather bloom,
    On the hills o' Caledonia.

My father's name, my father's lot,
Is now a tale that's heeded not,
Or sang unsung, if no forgot,
    On the hills o' Caledonia.
O' our great ha' there's left nae stane,
A' swept away like snaw lang gane;
Weeds flourish owre the auld domain
    On the hills o' Caledonia.

The Ti'ots' banks are bare and high,
The stream rins sma' an' mournfu' by,
Like some sad heart maist grutten dry,
    On the hills o' Caledonia.
The wee birds sing no frae the tree;
The wild flowers bloom no on the lea,
As if the kind things pitied me,
    On the hills o' Caledonia.

But friends can live, though cold they lie,
An' mock the mourner's tear an' sigh,
When we forget them, then they die,
    On the hills o' Caledonia.
An' howsoever changed the scene,
While mem'ry an' my feeling's green,
Still green to my auld heart an' een
    Are the hills o' Caledonia.

With trembling voice the first few words came
 forth,
Curbed half by bashfulness and half by fear,
Until the melody stole through her ears,
And opened wide the sluices of her heart.
'Twas then she gave to nature's hands the reins,
And tone and gesture in such union stirred,
As few could render, save the ancient bard
Who gave that song its birth.
                            The old man sat
And drank with thirsty ears the simple strain;
E'en when the maid had finished, sat he still,
And drank sweet thoughts the song had left
 behind.
At last he roused, and told that that sweet song
Was one out of a manuscript, the same
That we had seen him reading at the door,
Which manuscript to us did he hand o'er,
With leave to take it home and read it there.
"In truth," quoth he, "you'll find it full of thought,
Though rudely told; 'twas by a shepherd writ,
When on the hills he watched his woolly flock;
A man whom God had made for higher work.
He was my grandfather, and as good thoughts
And feelings fine came upward in his brain,
He let them fall on paper, so beguiled
The lazy hours that kept him on the hills."

Once more we left our seats, and took our leave
Of that old man whom we admired so much,
And after some hours' walk we reached our home.
At earliest leisure, this old manuscript,
(A poem was it, and "The Nobles" named,)
With some old songs appended to the end,
Did I scan o'er, and as our host had said,

Found I it true. 'Twas rude, constructed ill,
With language more uncouth than lacking fire ;
Yet did a kindly vein of nature flow
Throughout the work, mixed up with noble
 thoughts,
That, magnet-like, me to the author drew,
For profit and for pleasure.   To undertake
The rooting out of all the ancient words
That progress now has rendered obsolete ;
To frame anew, and give to it such dress
As modern taste requires, 'twas now my task ;
How far I have succeeded, Reader, judge.

ON THE DEATH OF ROBERT NICHOLL.

O Death ! ye play a mournfu' part,
Aye ready wi' your cursed dart
To strike the nearest, dearest heart—
 The noblest head,
Without a word to soothe the smart
 O' sic a deed.

Ye've stown away the sweetest breath,
That e'er in God or God's spak faith,
Wha ne'er gae pain in words o' skaith
 To auld or young ;
The very deevil wad been laith
 T'have stapp'd his song.

He watched the simple sheep an' kye,
The blooming flow'rs of every dye,

ON THE DEATH OF ROBERT NICHOLL.

The waters as they wimpled by
Thro' field or grove ;
The owre word o' his sang was aye
" God, let me love."

The birds nae sweeter sung than he,
While lying musing on the lea,
An' noting a' sweet things that be,
An' yearned to know ;
He felt his immortality
Within him grow.

An' ear sae true, a voice sae rare,
Ye might hae had the mense to spare ;
'Tis forty years syne, something mair,
Ye took his brother,
Puir Robbie Burns, now oh ! despair,
Ye've struck the other.

If ye'd been hungry after sport,
Why sought ye no the kirk or court,
Or mony other black resort,
O' names ill-faur'd ?
Where ye'd have had some pleasure for't,
The vile die hard.

Why sought ye no some tyrant's bed,
Whose page of life was nearly read,
Wi' black remorse in heart an' head,
To bursting cramm'd ?
What joy for you to nick his thread
An' ken him damn'd.

Or mony thousand mair forbye,
Wha lazy dozing round ye lie,
E'en fit for naething but to die
An' rot ; but na,
The mental great's the dainty fry
Maun stap your maw.

I mickle fear that ye hae been
Owre lang unto the killing gi'en,
To mak sic blunders as I've seen—
D'ye ever think ?
I hope my worthy, ancient frien',
Ye dinna drink.

But hark, ye dour destroying hind,
Auld scavenger o' human kind,
What pow'r hae ye owre human mind,
Tho' owre its clay?
Can ye touch that, howe'er inclined,
An' lang your day?

Our poet lives for a' your crooks,
Your winding sheets an' kirkyard neuks,
Whene'er we wish to scan his looks,
Sae free an' fair,
We've but to turn us to his books
An' see him there.

Whene'er we wish to hear his sang,
We've but to stroll the fields amang,
Or listen when the nights are lang,
An' wheels gang round,
Then is he heard in many a throng,
In many a sound.

Let college manufactured men,
Draw near an' trace his glowing pen,
He sings that learning's glorious when
It is o' use ;
But wasting time in idle ken,
Is great abuse.

List, sons o' mind in humble sphere,
He prays ye no to scorn nor fear,
But say your say in hamely lear,
The truth to a';
A thoughtfu' speech an' look sincere,
Let be your law.

Come gentle hearts that never hate,
Come heads that grow wi' thinking great,
Oh! mourn, oh! mourn, ye've lost a mate
To good men dear ;
While ye sit musing owre his fate,
His name revere.

PRAYER OF A COLOURED MAN.

Written on the Mississippi, May 1840.

GREAT Father of this beauteous earth,
Of beauteous worlds beside ;
How long shall tyranny have birth?
How long shall't o'er me ride?
Will time ne'er bring
A cheering spring?
Am I a slave, a soulless thing?

If I am doomed to live a slave,
To toil for pale mankind,
A crawling creature to the grave,
Oh! why have I a mind?
How long shall't steep
In moral sleep,
That when it wakes, but wakes to weep?

If I am doomed to live a slave,
Why have I a human form,
The form divine that nature gave?
Why rather not a worm,
Some creeping thing,
That bears the sting,
Yet knows not of its suffering?

If I am doomed to live a slave,
Let no fair flow'r or tree
Its blossoms spread or branches wave
In beauty before me;
But bloom confin'd
To human kind,
I cannot see—the brute is blind.

If I am doomed to live a slave,
Ne'er let affection cling
Around my heart, ne'er let me cleave
To wife, or child, or thing;
For what are ties
To him who lies
Chained even to the heart and eyes?

If I am doomed to live a slave,
Shut up my ears and tongue,
So I no moral sense may have

Of what is said or sung ;
But crawl along
Amid the throng
Untaught by speech, unfired by song.

If I'm *not* doomed to live a slave,
Let me not bow the knee,
Let him no more of mortal crave,
Whom thou createdst free ;
But if designed
For such a hind,
Great God ! pray take thou back my mind.

A PASSING QUESTION.

To whom place you a statue there,
That giant slab of stone ?
Methinks the virtue somewhat bare,
That lacks mouth not its own,
To note and tell
The tears that fell
At great Duke Cypher's funeral knell.

To whom place you a statue there ?
How loved the man his kind ?
If fell not full unto his share
As much of heart as mind,
Pile stone on stone,
His name hath flown
Before the maggots reach the bone.

How many in cathedrals be,
And all of marble white,
Appropriate to the purity
Of actions good and bright ;

Yet there behold
The virtues told,
Of those who lived for lust and gold.

The man full of Christ's nobleness,
Who yearns to all of good,
Who lifts from ignorance, distress,
The human multitude;
In mem'ry thrives,
Deathless survives,
Though statueless, a world of lives.

THOUGHT.

Though patrons shun my house and name,
Who tells me I am poor?
Though fashion trumpets not my fame,
And rank goes by my door;
Though ignorance my fortunes mar,
My mind shall never sink,
For nature made me greater far—
She bade me live and think.

The gold that drops from wealthy hands,
Feeds those on whom it falls,
And oft as hire for base commands
It feeds while it enthrals;
But thought is like the sun and air,
Twin blessings with the show'r,
It nurtures millions far and near,
And millions sing its pow'r.

The fool who stalks in titles clad,
By chance or knav'ry bought,
Who rates a nod of his weak head
As worth an age of thought;

Could he but see the brain in me,
And taste its common drink,
The burthen of his pray'r would be
For liberty to think.

Oh! poor are they who spend their pow'r
In sensual joys and strife,
I'll think more rapture in an hour,
Than they feel through a life.
Sweet thought's the she whom I adore,
Entwined by many a link,
God! what can I of thee crave more,
Do I not live and think?

LOVE'S CRUELTY.

Love, close those eyes, they pain me sore,
And rob this world of night;
For pity's sake pray gaze no more,
Or I must die with light.
Cease that sweet song if thou dost prize
Thy conscience victim free;
Oh! spare my ears if not my eyes,
I'm drunk with melody.

Most hearts with some benevolence pant
For those in sorrow deep;
But thou to poor me wilt not grant
Even a time to sleep.
If thou dost wish my life, pray take
At once eyes, ears and breath,
I'll murmur not for thy dear sake,
To die so sweet a death.

EVIDENCE OF LOVE.

Oh! why am I thus happy made?
Why beats my heart with joy?
Will this enchantment never fade,
This rapture never cloy?
Whene'er I wander near thy smiles,
My senses seem to rove;
Dear Maid, I fear they are the wiles
That lead us on to love.

If it be love, then let me live
For ever loving thee;
And life its saddest pangs may give
They'll never trouble me.
Leander loved not as will I,
Although he swam a sea;
I'll venture earth and sea and sky,
So my reward be thee.

PHILOSOPHY OF LOVE.

Ah! why thy face in sorrow clad?
Why wear that chiding look?
There's nothing, Love, to make thee sad
Within this little book;
For it is full of melting strains,
The strains thou lov'st to hear,
Then banish all those jealous pains,
They ill become my dear.

The poet surely stole his light
From thee in this array,
Yet has he ta'en an age to write
What thou speak'st every day.

Pray banish, Love, that chiding look
And turn thy face on me,
Although my eyes were on his book,
My heart was reading thee.

LOVE'S DYING.

If love can fade, let heavy life,
With love twin-cherished die,
So I may never feel the strife
That in my heart would lie.
I've loved thee long ; I've loved thee deep,
Without once changing hue,
My hours by day—my dreams in sleep
Are made of thoughts of you.

But surely love can never fade,
While life remains within ;
Could heaven ever thus have made
For man so great a sin ?
Take love away from human hearts,
From earth take sun and air,
And all the verdure that imparts
To it a face so fair.

The closing grave love cannot kill,
 Though it be dark and cold ;
Our souls can love as ardent still,
Souls die not, nor grow old.
To die is not to cease to love ;
Take love, and I am dead,
And all the pow'rs from heaven above
Shall no more raise my head.

TO MY CHILD THAT LIVETH STILL.

My baby, they say thou art gone,
Deep laid in the quiet grave,
And slumbering there all alone,
While young flowers over thee wave,
And pity, and tell
The fate that befell,
To some heart that loved a sweet baby as well.

My baby, they say thou art gone,
Gone e'en as the young flowers go,
When summer's warm rays are all flown,
And winter is bringing its snow,
And bloweth the wind
So rude and unkind;
But ha! thou hast left a sweet fragrance behind.

Well, let them say on, thou art gone,
'Tis only thy body has died;
They dream not there's something lives on.
Whatever the body betide.
How helpless are they
Who linger the prey
Of grief for the loss of some beautiful clay!

Again they repeat thou art gone;
How little know they of death!
Hear I not thy tremulous tone,
And feel on my cheek thy soft breath,
And gaze on thy smile?
Yet they all the while
Are telling thou'rt dead in the old church aisle.

My baby, they say thou art gone;
That I am in anguish and pain,
Yet how can they say I mourn on,
When thou liv'st in my warm brain,
And whispereth me,
As I do love thee,
To love all young things that in this world may be?

My baby, they say thou art gone;
But no, thou abidest yet,
And cheerest thy father alone,
Until his last sun shall set,
When heart, tongue, and eye
Shall spiritless lie;
Till then, my sweet baby, thou'lt droop not nor die.

THE BEGGAR AND HIS BROTHER.

GOOD friend, come wander down the vale,
For I am in the strain;
Now ope thy ears and give a tale
Free passage to thy brain,
For every tale its lesson brings,
To swell the human lore,
The poorest still can teach some things
The world knew not before.

I saw a man of many years
Stand begging by the way,
As o'er his cheeks escaping tears
Had not been shed alway.

His eyes were cast upon the ground,
His hat was in his hand,
And shining white hairs streamed around,
As begging he did stand.

There came a priest, with saintly eye
Upon the heavens bent,
Who often preached of charity
Unto those who want.
Yet was he blind to sorrow's tear,
Though livings had he three,
The beggar's words reached not his ear,
"Good sir, I pray your charity."

A statesman next passed onward, who
Gave laws unto the poor,
Who thought that law alone would do
To bless the poor man's door.
When hunger's pangs the poor assail,
Does law stay hunger's cry?
Yet passed he too the beggar's tale,
"Good sir, I pray your charity."

Another came, as mean as he,
The beggar who stood there,
Whose looks craved as much charity,
His garments were as bare.
Yet did he on the beggar gaze,
With kind and pitying eye,
For he had tasted better days,
And knew the bliss of charity.

He drew, while gazing on the ground,
A penny from his store;
A penny was to him a pound,
For, kind man, he was poor.

He thought of his old father, dead,
And what himself might be,
He gave the coin. The beggar said
"God bless, kind sir, your charity."

Now when I saw the joy to both
That penny did impart,
I said, behold in heaven's own truth,
Two children of one heart.
The giver was both sick and sad,
And poor as poor could be,
Yet did he make his brother glad;
God surely blessed his charity."

TRUTH.

Written after spending an evening with Allan Cunningham.

COME sit thee down, and we will sing
The thinking days of old,
And days that future times shall bring,
When we lie dead and cold.
We'll sing mind's winter and its spring,
In cottage and on throne,
How subject, king, and meaner thing,
Must kneel to truth alone.

We've read of man, in ages past,
When reason was a child,
His world the woods—his God the blast,
Untutored, poor, and wild.
Behold him now, in every sphere
Of intellectual skill;
'Tis truth that onward led him here,
And onward leads him stlil.

The mighty king who wears a crown,
From whom injustice flows—
How weak the hand can bring him down,
When truth directs the blows!
The peasant, scant of worldly gain,
Unletter'd tho', and rude,
While truth alone directs his brain,
He rises to a god.

From earth and water, sun and air
Sweet blessings on us fall;
But there is that, so bright and fair,
Reigns monarch of them all.
The sun without it were a blot;
Our lives a load of care:
The earth a bleak unsightly spot,
If truth resides not near.

Then let us look, and smile, and sing,
And think on our own way;
Our clay may rot—our souls take wing,
Truth never will decay.
'Twill live when this our world shall be
Perfection in its plan.
O Allan! should we that but see,
What could we wish for then?

VERSES WRITTEN AFTER HEARING "RULE BRITANNIA" SUNG.

O NEVER sing of ruling wide,
O'er earth and ocean's waves
It adds not to a nation's pride
To rise through others' graves.

CANDOUR.

The state for me is that which free
And ever kind does move,
With merry heart receives her part,
Not grasping, but in love.

Who grasps at more than he can fold
Must always lose his sway;
A hand can but a handful hold,
And more must slip away.
For every thing of heaven and earth
Within its limits move;
Kind nature sends the lesson forth,
Not grasping, but in love.

The winged birds keep them to the air;
The fish unto the sea;
The wild beast to the forest lair,
And all by God's decree.
Would rulers with their glory strive,
Like them in place to move,
Then men would live and men would thrive,
Not grasping, but in love.

CANDOUR.

SHALT thou give pain unto thy heart
By juggling with thy face;
Thy tongue and features be the part
Whereon thy feelings trace?
First think aright,
And day and night
Speak out in truth, as sun in light.

The truth's the truth, whoever he,
To whom the truth be told;
Let witlings rail and mock at thee,
Dull greybeards call thee bold.
Ne'er let them move
Thy ardent love
For all the truth that thou canst prove.

A CAUTION.

Pass by the maid without a heart,
Whate'er the wiles she use,
Her charms can ne'er to thee impart
What thou of peace may lose.
For joy ne'er thrives
With men and wives,
If love joins not their two dear lives.

A beauteous face is brief delight,
And often dearly bought;
Lips are not sweet—eyes are not bright,
If not the gates of thought;
But glass and clay,
For children's play,
The painted doll of one short day.

But she whose looks and thoughts are fair,
Woo her as for thy life,
For earth and heaven fall to thy share,
Combined in such a wife.
Earth's sweetest bliss
Lies in her kiss;
Her mind heaven's brightest loveliness.

TO MOURNERS.

Why mock thy friend with sighs and tears?
What weighs a garb of black?
The wailing of a thousand years
Will never bring him back.
Leave tears and sighs,
The common lies
Of grasping heirs when kindred dies.

If e'er thy friend dwelt in thy brain,
Why there resides he still,
In spite of that and all its train,
There's that death cannot kill.
The body may
Return to clay,
But mind blooms on through earth's decay.

Are not his thoughts and actions fast
Around thy feelings twined?
Then shame to say thy friend is lost,
When thou retain'st his mind;
While mem'ry hath
No loss of breath,
The dead can live and laugh at death.

TO MY PEN.

I cannot think, poor pen, not I,
To furnish food for thee,
My love is closely standing by
And robbing thee and me.
The thought that tries to struggle forth,
And give thy life its bliss,
She meets it as it reaches birth,
And kills it with a kiss.

As light departs from an eclipse,
So thought her presence flies,
For when she kills not with her lips,
She wounds it with her eyes.
Yet though she steals away my brain,
And leaves small sense with me,
Woo her for food, my poet pen,
She may be kind to thee.

LOVE.

WERE my dear love the balmy air,
And I this earth below,
Space I would drain though in it there
Were mingled every woe.
Were I yon golden sun so bright,
My love this fragrant plain;
Adieu for ever, murky night,
I'd never set again.

Had angels in the regions high
A shadow of her mind,
Oh! how poor man from sin would fly,
And leave the earth behind.
All forms that live between the poles,
Would heav'nward turn their eyes;
The very brutes would crave for souls,
And hie them to the skies.

A COMPANY.

THE hall was filled, the wine went round,
The wind blew loud and strong;
A knock was heard amid the sound
Of revelry and song.

One craved a shelter from the storm
That wildly raged without;
Bare was his garb, and weak his form,
His white hairs streamed about.

He pale and poor and cold did seem,
A wandering bard was he,
Whose life had been a troubled dream,
Half song, half misery.

They led him to a vacant seat,
The wine again went round;
The harp unstrung lay at his feet,
The guests they sat around.

"A song, Sir Bard," demanded one,
"And let it be the wars,
How we our thousand vict'ries won,
Our thousand wounds and scars!"

"I sing no songs that tell of wars,
Not one my budget yields,"
Replied the bard, "nor wounds nor scars,
Nor aught of battle-fields."

"Then sing of woman, let her be
One neither sad nor shy;
But ever ready, ever free,
Nor knows how to deny."

"Of woman list I not a song,
But what is pure and kind,
Unto whose loveliness belong
The graces of the mind."

Loud laugh'd the guests, and jeer and shout
Fell on the bard in show'rs,
And "Cast him out," came from the rout
Of those same revellers.

They thrust him forth unto the road,
The door was closed behind;
Below him was the wat'ry sod,
About him was the wind.

As jeer and shout came from the rout,
He thought, amid their din,
He was more at home with the storm without
Than with fellow-men within.

SONG OF A DRINKER.

THERE'S not a man this day alive
With heart so light as I:
I've numbered three-score years and five,
Yet know not how to sigh.
It never has been my sad lot,
To see Old Care come nigh,
Or if it has, I knew him not,
So pass'd the fellow by.

Though hoary hairs hang thin about
My brow and wrinkled skin,
I've that can mock the age without,
A fire burns bright within.
I laugh and quaff a brimming cup,
But, sirs, not filled with wine,
Wine never gave such pleasure up,
As can this cup of mine.

DEVOTION.

As I walk on by dell or hill,
  Or by the river's brink,
The cup is full before me still,
  Inviting me to drink.
I quaff until my old eyes wink,
  Then soars my spirit high,
And as I drink, and drink, and drink,
  More thirsty still grow I.

The nectar that breathes fire to me,
  From nature's bosom flows,
The beautiful of land and sea,
  Of every plant that grows.
The richest flavours, scents, and dyes,
  The clearest streams that run,
And all things sweet to hearts and eyes,
  Are in it—every one.

When my warm blood has ceased to flow,
  My bones beneath the stone,
Oh! may my soul walk here below,
  And drink as I have done.
Or if it must appear on high,
  By heaven's great decree,
I pray the cup may pass the sky
  Companion still with me.

DEVOTION.

I never knew that life was sweet,
  I never felt devotion,
Till my love's eyes did on me rise,
  As rays upon the ocean.

I thought that earth from an eclipse,
By magic had been riven;
And when I tasted her sweet lips,
Oh! then I murmur'd "Heaven!"

I've read of rev'rend sages who
Declaim against life's pleasures,
Who love's endearments never knew,
Nor dreamt of half its treasures;
Had they one glance of my love's e'e,
Farewell their holy faces,
Their only worship then would be,
The worship of her graces.

THE TUNE OF GALLA WATER.

Of tunes that with my heart accord,
There's not one love I better
Than that sweet song without a word,
The tune of Galla Water.

Though other songs may be as sweet,
Tunes and words together,
Yet while it speaks I feel my feet
Upon my native heather.

The more I list, the more the strain
Steals through my senses winning,
The last vibrated note again
Gives place to the beginning.

How warm the heart, from whence there sprung
A melody so feeling!
Alone could nature thus have sung,
For 'tis of her revealing.

Some rustic son of Scottish song,
Or maybe some fair daughter,
That caught it as it rose among
The banks of Galla Water.

The name, alas! I cannot show,
By guess, far less asserting;
But this in verity I know,
Beyond the controverting—

Of tunes that with my heart accord,
There's not one love I better,
Than that sweet song without a word,
The tune of Galla Water.

DEAR LOVE.

Dear Love, wilt thou go to the fields with me;
There wander away the day,
And revel in sweets like the joyous bee,
Till our senses are drunk away?
I'll show thee the father-like heaven above,
Feeding the earth below
In glittering streams of showers and beams,
The life of all things that grow;
I'll show thee the earth with her visage mild,
As she's seen from some gentle hill;
And looking as pleased as a laughing child,
When the young thing has had its will.

Then, Love, come with me,
To the flower and bee;
For love is most love when in company.

Dear Love, wilt thou go to the fields with me,
There wander away the day,
And revel in sweets like the honey bee,
Till our senses were drunk away?
I'll let thee, Love, hear the spirit of spring
Speaking among the trees,
From the throats of the hidden birds that sing
Beautiful melodies!
And the woods that appear so green and so fair,
And wear such a face of glee;
And we'll sing together in concert there
With the birds on the bush and the tree.
Then, Love, let us hie to where songs abound,
For oh! love is sweet when it's drunk in sound.

MY BOOKS.

SOME love to gaze on beauty's face,
And list to beauty's tongue;
Some age's looks and thoughts to trace,
And prattle with the young.
No face, nor tongue, nor youth, nor age,
Gives half the joy to me
That I can draw from one small page
Of what from cant is free,
     My Books.

They're not in rich morocco bound,
Nor writ in lettered gold;
On worldlings shelves are never found,
Nor ever look they old;

The hills, the streams, and fresh green fields,
The mountains, rocks, and trees,
And every scene that nature yields,
I ever find in these,
                    My Books.

END OF POEMS.

GLOSSARY.

A.

A', all.
Aboon, above, up.
Ae, one.
Aften, often.
Ain, own.
Aith, an oath.
Alane, alone.
Amaist, almost.
Amang, among.
An', and, if.
Ance, once.
Ane, one.
Anither, another.
Ase, ashes.
Auld, old.
Ava, at all.
Awa', away.
Awfu', awful
Ayont, beyond.

B.

Bairn, child.
Bairnies, children.
Baith, both.
Bardie, bard, poet.
Bauld, bold.
Birdie, bird.
Blate, bashful, sheepish.
Blaw, to blow, to boast.
Blink, a smiling look, a little while, to look kindly, to shine by fits.
Bonnie or *bonny*, handsome, beautiful.
Brae, a declivity, a precipice, the slope of a hill.
Brak, broke.
Braw, fine, handsome.
Bree, brow.
Breckan, fern.
Brither, a brother.
Bummin', humming as bees.
Burn, water, a rivulet.
But, *bot*, with.

C.

Ca', to call, to name.
Ca't, called.
Callan, a boy.
Caller, fresh, sound, refreshing.
Cantie or *canty*, cheerful, merry.
Carle, an old man.
Cauld, cold.
Chiel or *cheel*, a young fellow.
Claes or *claise*, clothes.
Claith, cloth.

GLOSSARY.

Claw, to scratch.
Coila, that district of Ayrshire in which Burns was born.
Coof, a blockhead, a ninny.
Couthie, kind, loving.
Crouse, cheerful, courageous.

D.

Dearie, my dear.
Dinna, do not.
Doo, dove.
Douce or *Douse*, sober, wise, prudent.
Doure, sullen, stubborn, stout.
Dowie, worn with grief.
Drift, a drove.
Drouthy, thirsty.
Dule, sorrow.

E.

E'e, the eye.
E'en, the eyes.
E'enin, evening.

F.

Fa', fall, lot, to fall.
Fa's, does fall, waterfalls.
Faes, foes.
Faut, fault.
Fearfu', frightful.
Fit, a foot.
Fleech, to supplicate in a flattering manner.
Flyte, scold.
Forbye, besides.
Forgather, to meet, to encounter with.
Forgie, to forgive.

Fou', full, drunk.
Frae, from.
Frien', friend.
Fu' full.

G.

Gae, to go.
Gaen, gone.
Gang, to go, to walk.
Gar, to make, to force to.
Gaucy, jolly.
Gear, riches, goods of any kind.
Ghaist, a ghost.
Gie, to give.
Gied, gave.
Gien, given.
Gin, if, against.
Glen, dale, deep valley.
Gaed, went.
Gowan, the flower of the daisy.
Gowd, gold
Grane, a groan, to groan.
Grannie, grandmother.
Greet, to shed tears, to weep.
Gude, the Supreme Being, good.

H.

Ha', hall.
Hae, to have.
Hame, home.
Hallan, a particular partition wall in a cottage, or more properly a seat of turf at the outside.
Hamely, homely, affable.
Himsel', himself.
Hiney, honey.

H

GLOSSARY.

I.

Ilk or *ilka*, each, every.

K.

Keek, a peep, to peep.
Ken, to know.
Ken'd or *ken't*, knew.
Kin, kindred.
Kist, a chest, shop-counter.
Knowe, a small round hillock.
Kye, cows.

L.

Laddie, lad.
Lan', land, estate.
Lane, lone, *my lane, thy lane*, myself alone, &c.
Lanely, lonely.
Lang, long, to think long, to long, to weary.
Lave, the rest, the remainder, the others.
Laverock, the lark.
Leal, loyal, true, faithful.
Lift, sky.
Lightly, sneeringly, to sneer at.
Lilt, a ballad, a tune, to sing.

M.

Mair, more.
Maist, most, almost.
Maistly, mostly.
Mak, to make.
Mang, among.
Maun, must.
Mavis, the thrush.
Mawin, mowing.

Mickle, much.
Min', mind, resemblance.
Mither, mother.
Morn, the next day, to-morrow.
Mou, the mouth.
Muckle or *mickle*, great, big, much.
Mysel', myself.

N.

Na', no, not, nor.
Nae, no, not any.
Naething, nothing.
Nane, none.
Neebor, neighbour.

O.

O', of.
Ony or *onie*, any.
Or, is often used for ere, before.
Owre, over, too.

P.

Pat, did put, a pot.
Pauky or *pawkie*, cunning, sly.
Poortith, poverty.
Pow, the head, the skull.
Pree, to taste, to kiss.
Preed, tasted.

R.

Rattan, rat.
Raw, a row.
Rin, to run, to melt, *rinning*, running.
Row, to roll, to wrap.

GLOSSARY.

S.

Sae, so.
Saft, sot.
Sair, to serve, a sore.
Sairly, sorely.
Saunt, a saint.
Saut, salt.
Sel', a body's self, one's self alone.
Serried or *Ser'd*, served.
Sin', since.
Slee, sly.
Sma', small.
Snaw, snow, to snow.
Snawie, snowy.
Sonsie, having sweet, engaging looks, lucky, jolly.
Spier, to ask, to inquire.
Stap, stop.
Stown, stolen.
Strae, straw.

T.

Tak, to take.
Takin, taking.
Tauld, told.
Thae, these.
Thrang, throng.
Through, to go on with, to make out.
Till't, to it.
Tine, to lose.
Toom, empty.
Twa, two.
'Twad, it would.

U.

Unco, strange, uncouth, very very great, prodigious.

W.

Wa', wall.
Wa's, walls.
Wad, would, to bet, a bet, a pledge.
Wadna, would not.
Wae, woe, sorrowful.
Waifu', wailing.
Wale, choice, to choose.
Warl' or *warld*, world.
Warly, worldly, eager on amassing wealth.
Wearie or *weary*, tired.
Wee, little.
Wee things, little ones.
Wee bit, a small matter.
Weel, well.
Wha, who.
Whare, where.
Whare e'er, wherever.
Whase, whose.
Whyles, wiles, sometimes.
Wi', with.
Wifie, an endearing term for wife.
Wimplin, waving, meandering.
Win', wind.
Win's, winds.
Winna, will not.
Woo, to court, to make love to.
Wrang, wrong, to wrong.

Y.

Ye, this pronoun is frequently used for you.
Yearns, longs much.
Year, is used for both singular and plural, years.
Yont, beyond.
Yoursel', yourself.

www.ingramcontent.com/pod-product-compliance
Lightning Source LLC
Chambersburg PA
CBHW020136170426
43199CB00010B/771